# Gordon Ramsay's
## Great Escape

# Gordon Ramsay's
# Great Escape

Food Mark Sargeant  Text Emily Quah  Photographer Emma Lee
Reportage Photography Jonathan Gregson  Art Director Patrick Budge
Props Stylist Emma Thomas

HarperCollins*Publishers*

## Cook's notes

Spoon measures are level, unless otherwise specified:
1 tsp is equivalent to 5ml; 1 tbsp is equivalent to 15ml.

Use good-quality sea salt, freshly ground pepper and fresh herbs for the best flavour.

Use large eggs unless otherwise suggested, ideally organic or free-range. If you are pregnant or in a vulnerable health group, avoid dishes using raw egg whites or lightly cooked eggs.

Individual ovens may vary in actual temperature by 10° from the setting, so it is important to know your oven. Use an oven thermometer to check its accuracy.

Timings are provided as guidelines, with a description of colour or texture where appropriate, but readers should rely on their own judgement as to when a dish is properly cooked.

10 9 8 7 6 5 4 3 2 1

HarperCollins*Publishers*
77–85 Fulham Palace Road,
Hammersmith, London W6 8JB
www.harpercollins.co.uk

First published by HarperCollins*Publishers* 2010

Text © 2010 Gordon Ramsay
Food Photography © 2010 Emma Lee
Reportage Photography © 2010 Jonathan Gregson

A CIP catalogue record of this book is available from the British Library

ISBN 978-0-00-726705-7

Printed and bound in Italy by L.E.G.O. SpA

**Mixed Sources**
Product group from well-managed forests and other controlled sources
www.fsc.org  Cert no. SW-COC-1806
© 1996 Forest Stewardship Council
FSC

FSC is a non-profit international organisation to promote the responsible management of the world's forests. Products carrying the FSC label are independently certified to assure consumers that they come from forests that are managed to meet the social, economic and ecological needs of present and future generations.

Find out more about HarperCollins and the environment at www.harpercollins.co.uk/green

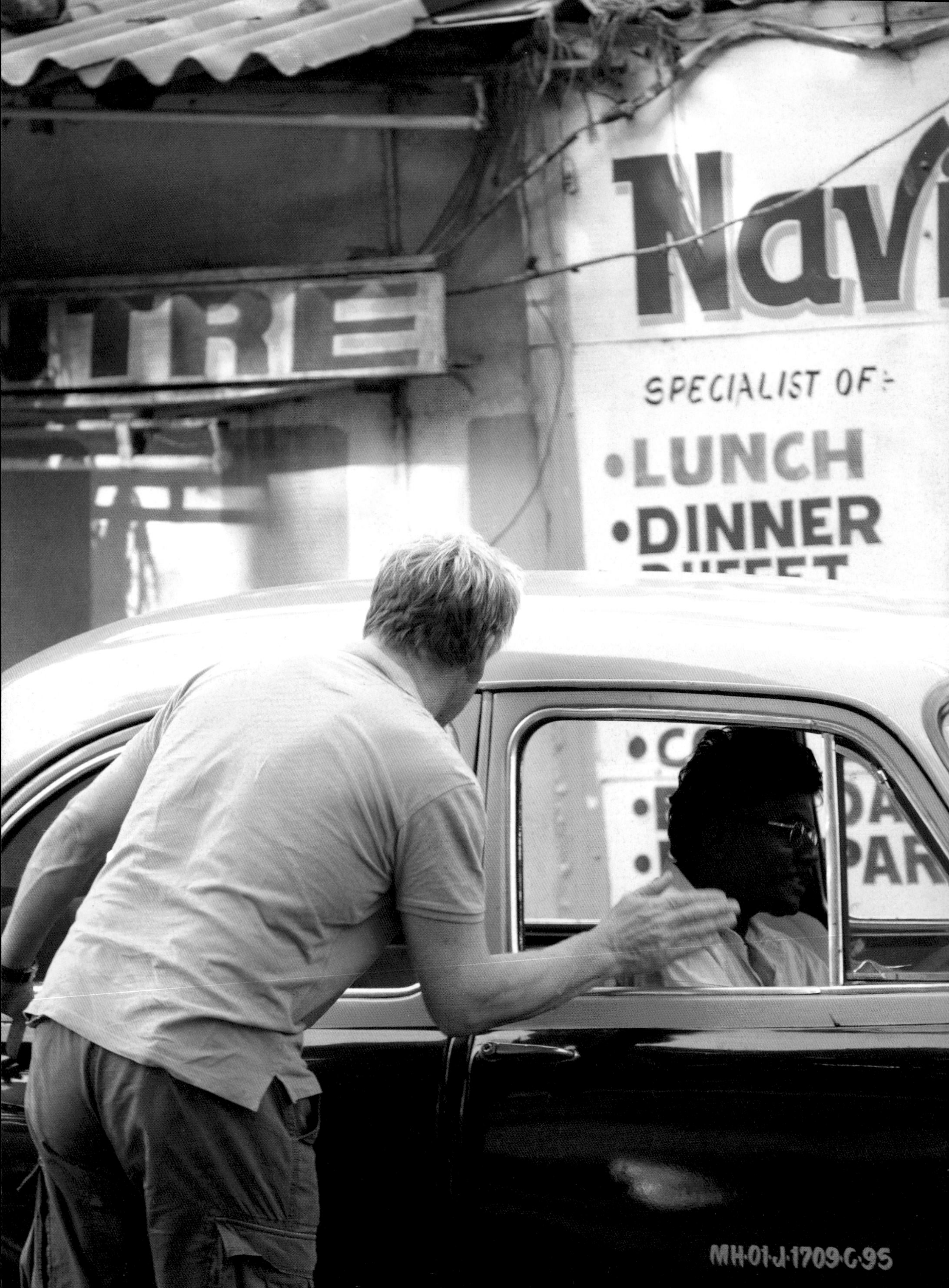
SPECIALIST OF:-
•LUNCH
•DINNER
MH-01-J-1709-C-95

# Contents

Since I left home and started working, Friday-night curries have become a ritual. Like most people, I have had favourite dishes, which I would order time and again, but overall I felt pretty comfortable with the food and thought that I knew quite a bit about Indian cuisine. How wrong I was! I had never been to India before this trip, and what little I knew about the country and its food was based on general stereotypes and preconceptions. I now realise that it is impossible to summarise the food of a vast subcontinent where differing cultures, religion, topography, climate and history all influence what food is eaten and how it is cooked.

When the opportunity came for a culinary adventure in India, the choice was simple. This was the chance of a lifetime to escape from the grind of daily life and discover the truth about Indian cuisine. I knew that real Indian food was not to be found in fancy restaurants and hotel eateries; instead I had to travel the country and eat as ordinary Indians do, regardless of caste, class or religious differences.

My journey started in the north, in the capital of New Delhi, home to 17 million residents. As I entered the city the first thing that struck me was the sheer contrast of wealth and severe poverty that was apparent everywhere, but I soon noticed that no matter what the individual situation was, almost everyone had a beaming smile. The Delhi residents also seemed to be working constantly, day and night; however, amid the hustle and bustle, I got a real sense of organised chaos that I had never experienced anywhere else before. In fact, this was the feeling I got in almost every Indian city to which I travelled, but Old Delhi was certainly a culture shock. The sights at the Red Fort were wonderful, and there were beautiful temples everywhere you looked, but, in the middle of it all, I was amazed to see rows of fragile-looking shacks that sold everything from mobile phones and shoes to food and Honda motorbikes!

Navigating and crossing the streets of Delhi proved to be a big challenge. The roads were filled with maniacs who drove wherever they chose with utter disregard for any street signs, regulations or pedestrians! There was a constant echo of horns beeping the whole time as every driver felt that he had the right of way. For me, the most amusing sight had to be the occasional herd of cows meandering along the streets, oblivious to oncoming traffic, while taxis, cars, motorbikes and tuk tuks did their best to avoid hitting the sacred animals.

Where food was concerned, my most memorable meal in Delhi was at the legendary Moti Mahal restaurant in Daryaganj, where classics such as tandoori chicken and butter chicken (one of my all-time favourites) were invented over 60 years ago. It was here that I met Seema Chandra, a renowned food writer and critic, who explained to me that the food in India is truly different from the Indian food that you get in Britain. This was clearly evident in the dishes at Moti Mahal: the delicious butter chicken was very moist, tender and flavoursome – unlike anything I've ever tasted. According to Seema, real Indian food is found on the streets and in family homes. Indians have not historically had a big restaurant culture, although this has now changed, and (for those who can afford it) eating out has become a popular pastime. Many homes have servants or mothers and grandmothers who prepare fresh, delicious meals for the entire family three times a day. Workers who do not have time to go home for lunch pick up cheap, delicious street food to sustain them until they can get home for dinner; children bring their lunches to school carefully packed in multi-tiered tiffin carriers, and shoppers indulge in street snacks before going home for their main meals. This emphasis on traditional home cooking means that recipes have been passed down from generation to generation and have seldom been well recorded, so if I wanted to get a true flavour of Indian cookery, I needed to roll up my sleeves and get my hands dirty.

One of the first things I learnt was that food is very important in India. Even the very poor will find a way to eat well with cheap but delicious meals. I understood this on board the Mangalore Express, on my way to Lucknow, the foremost city of food and culture. To earn my fare I was given an apron and immediately set on the task of prepping vegetables in the train cafeteria. There, a team of five chefs and 20 waiters make and serve fresh meals to over 400 passengers each day. For an equivalent of £110 a month, the chefs work 10 hours a day, 6 days a week in the most challenging of work environments. Pots constantly rattled and the portable stove shifted with the movements of the train. Nonetheless, they took great care to produce

hot, tasty and satisfying meals for the masses – a far cry from the pitiful, factory-made train food we have in the UK.

Lucknow was another revelation in terms of food. The city is famous for its exquisite cuisine and it is known as the birthplace of the korma and biryani. The original korma is a totally different dish from the British version, made lighter with yoghurt instead of cream and thickened with a paste made from ground almonds instead of coconut milk. The resulting dish was absolutely delicious, but it was a dark brownish-red colour instead of the creamy yellow to which we are accustomed. More remarkable were the biryanis, served at every festival and celebration. I had the privilege of spending a day with master chef, Imtiaz Qureshi, who in his heyday had catered for over 50,000 guests for a single event. We cooked *dum ba biryani*, a complex dish sophisticated enough to serve emperors and maharajahs. Similar in concept to a three-bird roast, this dish entailed two whole goats, four chickens and four quails stuffed with saffron-marinated quails' eggs. The stuffed goats were then placed on a bed of biryani rice and meatballs, and the cooking pot was sealed with pastry to capture the aromatic flavours of the dish as it was finished off. A truly amazing biryani that you are unlikely to find in any cookery book (so I just had to include it in this one, see page 179)!

After experiencing the rich and indulgent food of the north, I went in search of back-to-basics cooking, and in unfamiliar territories. My travels took me to the poor, remote district of Bastar in the central state of Chhattisgarh. Here the local speciality is *chakra*, a delicious hot and tangy chutney made with chopped red chillies, salt, ground fresh ginger and a secret key ingredient: local ants! For obvious reasons I haven't included the recipe in this book, but the local tribe has taught me what it really means to live off the resources of the land. Every single ingredient is sourced locally, and with the lack of refrigeration there is a strong emphasis on fresh produce.

This simple and honest approach to food was echoed in Nagaland and Assam, two of the Seven Sister States I visited in the remote northeastern corner of India. Dried spices, so ubiquitous in mainstream Indian cooking, are virtually absent from recipes there; instead, fresh chillies, ginger and garlic are the predominant flavourings. Meat and fish are hunted and cooked on the bone, resulting in very little wastage, and every part of an animal is eaten. I was also intrigued by the prevalent use of bamboo shoots in Nagaland, both in the fresh, smoked and dried forms, which link the cuisine to those of neighbouring China and Myanmar. Naturally, rice is the staple food of the region, and it comes in various forms. A local favourite is glutinous rice roasted in segments of fresh bamboo over an open fire. Talk about low-impact eco-cooking!

Next, my travels took me to the coastal areas of Kerala. With its beautiful and lush waterways, it is a much calmer and more relaxed part of India – exactly what I needed after an exhausting couple of weeks criss-crossing the country. Naturally, rice and fish are their staples, but as there is a sizeable Syrian Christian population in the area, pork and beef were also back on the menu. The food is lighter, as coconut milk is used in place of butter and cream, and more fragrant with the liberal use of spices and fresh curry leaves. One of the tastiest dishes I tried was *karimeen pollichathu* (see page 70). Karimeen is a much loved local freshwater fish, dubbed the 'Fish of Kerala', and in this dish it is smothered with a spice paste and roasted in banana leaves. The fish had a sublime flavour that reminded me of a sweet Dover sole; it is a real shame we can't get it in England.

No trip to Kerala is complete without a visit to a spice market, and I was extremely impressed with the multi-coloured markets of Cochin. The image of giant piles of ginger, turmeric, cinnamon, cardamom and saffron (as well as the intoxicating fragrance) will always be embedded

in my memory. Standing in the middle of the market was a defining moment for me, it was then that I realised that one of the most important things to learn about Indian cooking is the delicate art of spicing. Although the use of various spices differs according to the region, religious beliefs or simply personal preference, the creative use of spice is what binds all Indian food together. Indian dishes may not always blow your head off in terms of heat (although many will), but they will always be fragrant and flavourful. The secret is in understanding how to draw out the natural flavours of a spice or change its characteristic and basic flavour profile – either through frying in oil, dry roasting or grinding – and using it to enhance the central ingredients of a dish. Spice combinations cannot be taught; you have to taste and experiment as you go along and learn from trial and error.

My culinary adventure ended in Mumbai (formerly known as Bombay), the capital of India. The city is such a key economic and cultural hub that nearly 200 different languages or dialects are spoken throughout the metropolis. At first glance it was disheartening to see the vast, seemingly never-ending stretches of slums surrounding the city. (Apparently, 55 per cent of the city's population lives in shanty-towns or slums.) On closer inspection, however, it was amazing to see a thriving community working and living within the buildings with their corrugated-iron roofs. I spent a day in the Dharavi slum, home to more than a million people, learning how to make *sambar* from an enterprising chef and caterer aptly called Sambar Mani. Sambar is a classic lentil and vegetable dish that is delicious, light and nourishing (see page 213). It is one of the most loved vegetarian dishes in South India, and it is eaten with either plain rice or steamed fermented rice cakes called *idli*. I was truly impressed with the care and attention to detail that went into making the sambar. Most importantly, the dish tasted fantastic (even to a die-hard carnivore like myself) and is far superior to any vegetarian food we have in Britain. My wife, Tana, has been trying to get the family to have a meat-free day once a week, and with food like this I'm sure she would come up with little resistance.

My final challenge, the culmination of this whole trip, was to cook a southern Indian feast for 25 high-society guests at the Taj Mahal Palace Hotel in Mumbai. As many people will remember, the hotel was badly bombed and attacked by terrorists in 2008. It was amazing to see how they have bounced back after such a terrible show of aggression, and what I found there was a passionate and thriving business. I decided to cook a trio of karimeen dishes for the main course. (One of the benefits of doing a television programme is that I had the luxury of being able to have fish flown in from Kerala.) The dishes were made with Indian spicing, of course, but with slight European twists in the cooking methods. I was glad that the guests loved the food, but on a personal level I felt that I had come full circle.

I may not have covered every classic dish of every region during my relatively short culinary tour (indeed this book contains some recipes that were simply inspired by my travels and some of these classic dishes), but the knowledge that I have gained from the trip is immense. I am truly grateful to all those people who entertained, inspired and put up with me during what was, I can safely say, the most exciting thing I have ever done. India is a place of passion – both for food and for life. The cuisine is reflective of the people and culture, which is wonderful, vibrant and multi-faceted. I will never forget my time in this incredible country, and I can't wait to return.

# Glossary

**Ajwain** – Also known as carom seeds, ajwain resemble small cumin seeds but they have a strong fragrance of thyme and a slightly bitter and pungent flavour. They are always roasted in the oven or fried in oil or butter in Indian cooking.

**Amchur/Amchoor** – Green mango powder made by grinding pitted unripe mangoes that have been left to dry out in the sun. It has a greyish colour and a distinctive tart flavour, hence its use as a souring agent for food. It does not require cooking but may be added to dishes or sprinkled over snacks in place of lemon juice or vinegar.

**Asafoetida** (*Hing*/*Heeng* in Hindi) – A spice made from the resinous gum of the *Ferula assafoetida* plant. Mostly sold in powdered form, asafoetida is used in tiny quantities as a digestive aid to fight off indigestion and flatulence. It is often added to dishes at the beginning of the cooking process to be cooked out with other spices. Raw asafoetida has a very pungent, rather disagreeable odour that seems to disappear once cooked to leave a mellow, slightly sweet tang that is similar to that of roasted onions and garlic. Because it is not widely sold in super-markets and you would only use a pinch in any dish, I have made it optional in the recipes here.

**Atta/Chapatti flour** – A wholewheat flour rich in fibre and protein that is used to make many classic unleavened Indian breads, such as chapatti and paratha. It can be bought from specialist Indian shops and some major supermarkets. If you can't find it, use equal quantities of wholemeal and plain flours.

**Chaat masala** – A dry spice blend with a distinctive sour flavour that is mostly used as a condiment. It is often sprinkled over Indian snacks, raw fruit salads and tandoori dishes, and it can also be used to 'liven' up fruit juices. The specific blend of spices may vary according to the brand (or individual tastes) but chaat masala usually consists of dried mango powder, dried ginger, black salt, ground dried mint and asafoetida. Ready-made packets are widely available at Asian grocers.

**Chai** – A generic Hindi word for tea, but outside of India chai is commonly used to imply masala chai, a popular Indian-spiced milk tea.

**Channa dal** – Also known as *cholar dal* in Bengali, these are skinned and split black gram – they look and taste similar to yellow split peas, but the grains are marginally smaller. They have an earthy and nutty flavour. If you can't get hold of them, use yellow split peas instead.

**Coconut oil** – An oil used commonly in southern Indian cooking that has been extracted from coconuts by a process of distillation. It is white in colour when solid but becomes transparent when heated. It has a high burning point, which makes it suitable for frying foods. It is high in saturated fats, and so for health reasons some people prefer to substitute it with other vegetable oils.

**Garam masala** – An aromatic spice blend that is used both during the cooking process, for a subtle fragrance, and as a garnish, where it is lightly sprinkled over a finished dish to give an added burst of aroma and flavour. *Garam* means 'warming' or 'hot' and the blend commonly includes cardamom seeds, cumin or black cumin seeds, nutmeg, black peppercorns, cloves and cinnamon, coriander and fennel seeds, although recipes vary significantly from region to region. Ready-made garam masala is easily found in supermarkets and Asian shops, but some brands tend to bulk up the ingredients with cheaper spices such as ground cumin and coriander.

**Ghee** – This is essentially clarified butter, which features heavily in northern Indian cooking. You can buy it ready-made in tins at Asian grocers, but I find these have a strong, overpowering aroma. To clarify butter, melt it gently, then pour off the oil through a muslin-lined sieve and discard the milky solids. For health reasons, many Indians now mainly cook with vegetable oil, but they will add a little unsalted butter or ghee to flavour and enrich a dish.

**Gram flour** – Also known as *besan*, this is made from finely ground chickpeas or channa dal. It is used in Indian cooking for a variety of purposes, such as soups and curries, and it is an integral part of the batter for bhajis and pakoras.

**Grated coconut** – Freshly grated coconut is often called for in Indian cooking. To extract the flesh from a coconut, crack it with the back of a strong cleaver or using a hammer. Drain off the coconut water (or save to drink later). You should have two halves of the coconut. Prise out the white flesh with a strong spoon then finely shred or grate using a food processor. Grated coconut can be frozen successfully for at least a month.

**Jaggery** – An unrefined natural sugar made from the concentrated sap of the date palm. It lends a distinctive sweet taste to both sweet and savoury dishes. Usually sold in solid blocks, jaggery is often grated before it is incorporated into dishes. The darker the colour of the jaggery, the stronger the flavour. You can substitute it with palm sugar or light brown soft sugar.

**Kalonji** – Also known as nigella seeds, these are black onion seeds with a tear-drop shape. Kalonji is frequently used in pickles, chutneys and fish dishes as well as sprinkled on to Indian flat breads.

**Karahi** – A large, all-purpose rounded pan that is an essential piece of equipment in an Indian kitchen. It is particularly useful for deep-frying as it allows you to use less oil than you would when using a regular saucepan. If you do not already own a karahi, a wok makes a very good substitute.

**Mustard oil** – The oil extracted from mustard seeds, this has a pungent and slightly bitter taste when raw. Once heated, it develops a distinctive sweet flavour. An acquired taste, it is most commonly used in Bengali cooking for pickling and cooking fish and vegetables. If you can't find it, substitute it with vegetable or groundnut oil.

**Panch phoran** – A Bengali spice blend made up of equal quantities of whole fennel seeds, fenugreek seeds, black mustard seeds, cumin seeds and nigella or black onion seeds.

**Paneer** – This fresh, unsalted curd cheese is widely used in both sweet and savoury Indian dishes. Paneer is very easy to make, requiring only whole milk and either lemon juice or vinegar. The milk is heated almost to boiling point, then removed from the heat and a little lemon juice or vinegar is stirred in. The milk will curdle or separate, and at this point the liquid is strained and hung for a few hours to remove the watery whey, leaving behind the fresh curd. Paneer is best made on the day it is to be eaten.

**Rosewater** – Made from distilled rose petals, rosewater is produced as a by-product of the process used to make rose oil. The widespread use of rosewater in Indian cooking comes from Persian influence; it is commonly sprinkled over biryani or pilau rice to lend a perfumed aroma to the dish.

**Tamarind** – Used as a souring agent in Indian cooking, particularly in the south, tamarind pulp is usually sold in blocks. To get tamarind purée, soak the tamarind pulp in water (roughly double the volume of water to weight of pulp) for at least 30 minutes. You should break the tamarind block up with your hands to achieve maximum flavour before straining the purée through a sieve and discarding the husks. More convenient but less flavour-some ready-made tamarind paste is now widely sold in jars in major supermarkets.

**Tuvar dal** – Dark ochre-coloured split and skinned pigeon pea lentils with a mild nutty and earthy flavour. These versatile lentils are very popular in Indian cooking and are a good source of protein and fibre.

**Urad dal** – Black gram usually sold split and skinned to reveal the yellow lentils inside. Urad dal is ground with rice to make the classic southern Indian dosa. It is also often fried in small quantities to give a nutty crunch to vegetable or rice dishes.

# Starters & snacks

Malai chicken kebabs

Galouti kebabs

Paneer tikka kebabs

Spiced tomato and coconut soup

Spicy prawn pakoras

Prawn koftas

Maharashtrian white bean patties

Lamb, cumin and mint samosas

Mixed vegetable samosas

Aubergine bhajis

Bombay potato cakes

Cottage cheese and sweetcorn fritters

Spicy vegetable and paneer wraps

Aloo dahi puri

# Malai chicken kebabs

These Punjabi chicken kebabs come from the north-west of India and are traditionally cooked in a hot tandoor. The kebabs are fairly mild, which makes them suitable for serving to a young family. To turn them into a main meal, serve with fluffy basmati rice or soft flat breads such as *puri* or *naan*, a sweet and sour chutney and some side vegetable dishes.

Cut the chicken into 2.5–3cm cubes. In a large bowl, mix together all the ingredients for the marinade and season well with salt and pepper. Add the chicken pieces to the marinade and mix well to ensure that every piece is well coated. Cover the bowl with cling film and chill for a few hours, preferably overnight.

Soak 6–8 bamboo skewers in cold water for at least 20 minutes. When ready to cook, heat the grill to the highest setting. Halve the peppers and remove and discard the seeds. Cut the peppers into small cubes the same size as the chicken pieces. Thread the chicken pieces and peppers alternately on to the soaked bamboo skewers and place on a lightly oiled baking tray. Grill for about 8–10 minutes, basting, turning and basting again with the ghee or butter a couple of times during cooking. The chicken should be just firm when lightly pressed.

Serve the chicken kebabs on shredded lettuce leaves with a few lemon wedges and a raita on the side.

**SERVES 4–6**
500g boneless and skinless chicken breasts
sea salt and freshly ground black pepper
6–8 bamboo skewers
1 red pepper
1 yellow or orange pepper
2 tbsp ghee or melted unsalted butter

**MARINADE**
150ml double cream or soured cream
2 cardamom pods, split and seeds finely crushed
3cm ginger, peeled and finely grated
3 large garlic cloves, peeled and finely crushed
2 tbsp gram flour
1 tsp garam masala
1 tsp dried mango powder
1 tsp ground cumin
½ tsp ground turmeric
2 mild green chillies, deseeded and finely chopped

**SERVES 4–5**

500g minced lamb leg

1 tsp grated ginger

2 tbsp chopped
coriander leaves
and stems

¼ tsp ground cloves

¼ tsp ground cinnamon

¼ tsp ground mace

1 cardamom pod,
seeds ground

1 tsp hot chilli powder,
or to taste

2 tbsp ground almonds

pinch of saffron strands

2 tbsp fresh pineapple
juice (or finely grated
raw papaya)

1 tsp rosewater

sea salt and freshly
ground black pepper

2 tbsp ghee or melted
unsalted butter

1 large onion, peeled
and finely chopped

3–4 tbsp gram (or plain)
flour

2 tbsp vegetable oil

# Galouti kebabs

*Galouti* means 'melt in the mouth', and these delicious lamb patties come from Uttar Pradesh, a region renowned for its kebabs. Good-quality minced lamb is marinated with ground spice and fresh pineapple juice or grated raw papaya, which contain enzymes that tenderise the meat. I like to serve the kebabs on warm naan breads with Spicy green chutney (see page 215), sliced onions, and tomatoes and cucumbers lightly dressed with lemon juice.

Put the lamb in a large mixing bowl with the ginger, coriander, ground spices, chilli powder and ground almonds. Soak the saffron in the pineapple juice for a few minutes, then add to the lamb mixture with the rosewater and some salt and pepper. (If using grated raw papaya, soak the saffron in a little milk or water instead.) Mix well with your hands, if you find it easier. Cover the bowl with cling film and chill.

Heat the ghee or butter in a saucepan. Add the onion and season, then cook, stirring occasionally, for 6–8 minutes until the onion is soft and translucent but not browned. Take the pan off the heat and leave to cool completely. Once cooled, add the cooked onion to the lamb and mix well. To check for adequate seasoning, fry off a teaspoonful of the mixture to taste. Cover the bowl again and chill for another 4–5 hours or overnight.

Shape the lamb mixture into 15–16 small patties with damp hands, then lightly coat each patty in gram flour. Heat the oil in a wide, non-stick frying pan and fry the patties in several batches for about 2–2½ minutes on each side until golden brown, keeping each batch warm in a low oven. Enjoy the kebabs while they are still hot.

# Paneer tikka kebabs

This quick snack requires little effort and the paneer provides a great source of protein for vegetarians. Most Indian households would make their own paneer, as the process is really simple, but many UK supermarkets now sell it ready-made in convenient blocks. Tandoori food, under which these kebabs are classified, are best cooked in the traditional, hot, domed tandoor oven to create a smoky flavour, but for domestic cooking a griddle pan, barbecue or a searing hot grill can be used to create similar results.

Soak 6 bamboo skewers in cold water for at least 20 minutes. Tip the paneer cubes into a large bowl along with the onion and pepper cubes. In a small bowl, mix together all the ingredients for the marinade until evenly combined. Pour the marinade over the paneer and vegetables and mix well. If you have time, leave them to marinate in the fridge for at least 30 minutes.

Thread the paneer on to the soaked skewers, alternating with the onion and pepper chunks. Heat a lightly oiled griddle pan until hot (or preheat the grill to the highest setting). Griddle or grill the skewers for 3–5 minutes on each side, basting with ghee or melted butter several times, until they are deliciously smoky and charred at the edges.

Serve straight away with some warm naan or chapatti breads and some Spicy green or Sweet tamarind chutney (see pages 215 and 217).

**MAKES 6**
6 bamboo skewers
225g paneer, cut into 2.5cm cubes
1 large onion, peeled and cut into 2.5cm cubes
1 red pepper, cored, deseeded and cut into 2.5cm cubes
2 tbsp ghee or melted unsalted butter

**MARINADE**
2.5cm ginger, peeled and finely grated
½ tsp hot chilli powder, or to taste
1 tsp carom seeds
1 tsp dried mango powder
1 tsp ground cumin
1 tsp garam masala
½ tsp fine sea salt
1 tbsp gram flour
100ml thick natural yoghurt

# Spiced tomato and coconut soup

**SERVES 4**

500g tomatoes
2 tbsp vegetable oil
1 large onion, peeled
  and chopped
2.5cm ginger, peeled
  and chopped
2 large garlic cloves,
  peeled and chopped
sea salt and freshly
  ground black pepper
2 red chillies, deseeded
  and finely chopped
½ tsp dried fenugreek,
  crushed with a pinch
  of salt
1 bay leaf
1 tsp ground turmeric
1 tsp ground cumin
100g tomato purée
400ml tin coconut milk
pinch of sugar (optional)
1 tbsp coconut or
  vegetable oil
1 tsp cumin seeds
pinch of asafoetida
  (optional)
handful of coriander
  leaves and 2 tbsp
  toasted flaked coconut,
  to garnish (optional)

This is my take on *rasam*, a spicy South Indian tomato soup, which is generally served with rice as a second course, following an appetising dish of *sambar* (see page 213). It is thought that our much loved mulligatawny soup is a derivative of rasam, although we have, through the years, toned down the heat level to suit tamer British palates. For this soup, it is better to use cheap cooking tomatoes that are flavourful but slightly sour, as this provides an astringency to balance the slightly sweet and creamy coconut milk.

Bring a pan of water to the boil. Lightly score a cross at the top and base of each tomato then lower them into the boiling water for 15–20 seconds. Remove with a slotted spoon and refresh in a bowl of iced water. Once cooled, peel off the skins of the tomato and roughly chop the flesh. Set aside.

Heat the oil in a medium saucepan and add the onion, ginger and garlic. Add a pinch of salt and some pepper and sweat for 4–5 minutes until the onion begins to soften. Add the chillies, fenugreek, bay leaf, turmeric and cumin and cook for another 3–4 minutes. Tip in the chopped tomatoes and tomato purée and stir well.

Pour in the coconut milk and use the tin to measure out an equal amount of water. Add this to the pan and bring to a simmer. Cook gently for about 15–20 minutes until the tomatoes are very soft and have broken down.

Purée the soup using a stick blender (or an ordinary one) and if you want a really smooth result, push the purée through a fine sieve into a clean pan. Season well to taste with salt and black pepper, adding a pinch of sugar if it tastes too acidic from the tomatoes. If you prefer a thinner soup, dilute it with some boiling water and adjust the seasoning.

When you are ready to serve, reheat the soup. In a small saucepan, heat the coconut or vegetable oil and add the cumin seeds and asafoetida, if using. As they begin to pop, take the pan off the heat and pour the spiced oil into the tomato soup. Stir well.

Ladle into warm bowls and garnish with coriander leaves and toasted flaked coconut, if you wish. Serve immediately.

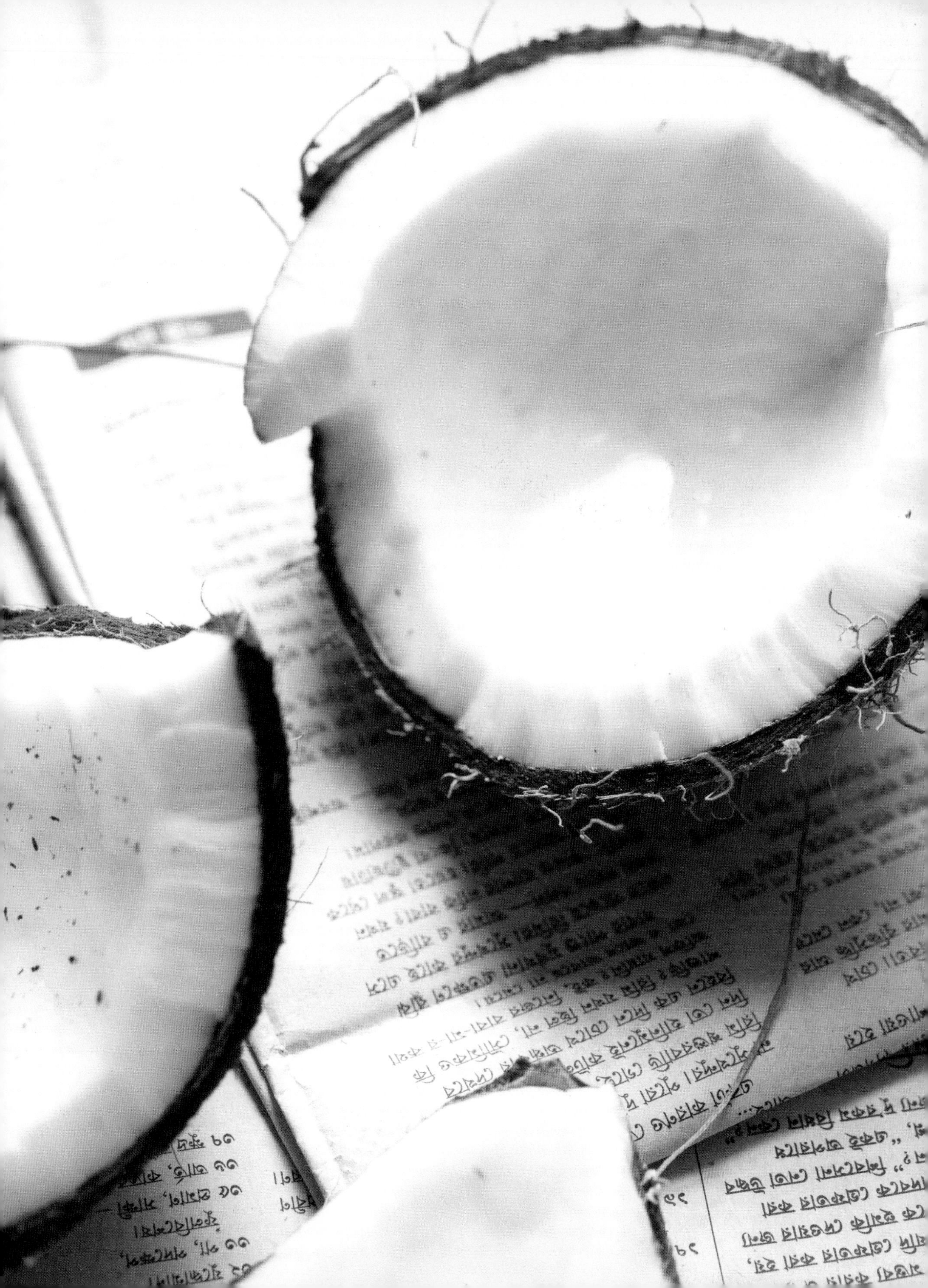

# Spicy prawn pakoras

I like to think of pakoras as the Indian equivalent of the Japanese tempura. They typically consist of fish, meat or vegetables that are coated in a batter made from spiced gram (chickpea) flour and then deep-fried until golden brown. These prawn pakoras are especially delicious with a Spicy green or Tomato and cucumber chutney (see pages 215 and 224).

Shell and devein the prawns, leaving the tails intact. Place them in a bowl and toss with the chopped chillies and garlic.

Next, make the batter by mixing the flour, salt and spices together in a large bowl. Make a well in the centre and add just enough of the warm water to form a thick, smooth paste with a slow-dropping consistency. Leave to stand for a few minutes.

Preheat the oven to the lowest setting and heat 6cm of oil in a karahi or deep saucepan to 170–180ºC. One at a time, hold the prawns by their tails, dip them in the spicy batter mix to coat, then drop them into the hot oil. Fry for 3–4 minutes, turning once, until crisp and golden brown all over. Drain on a baking tray lined with kitchen paper and keep warm in the oven while you cook the rest. Serve immediately while they are still hot.

**SERVES 4**

350g raw prawns, shell on
2 green chillies, deseeded and very finely chopped
3 garlic cloves, peeled and finely crushed
vegetable oil, for deep-frying

**BATTER**

150g gram (or plain) flour
½ tsp sea salt
½ tsp ground turmeric
½ tsp cumin seeds
½ tsp ground coriander
½ tsp garam masala
100–125ml warm water

**SERVES 4**

450g prawns, peeled
  and deveined
sea salt and freshly
  ground black pepper
handful of coriander
  leaves and stalks
2 medium onions,
  peeled and very finely
  chopped
2 green chillies,
  deseeded and finely
  chopped
75g dried breadcrumbs
vegetable oil, for
  shallow-frying

**SAUCE**

1 tbsp vegetable oil
20g unsalted butter
1 large onion, peeled
  and finely chopped
3cm ginger, peeled and
  finely grated
2 tsp garam masala
1 heaped tsp ground
  turmeric
400ml tin coconut milk
150ml water

# Prawn koftas

These delectable prawn koftas are served with a lightly spiced sauce, which is delicious soaked up with warm flat breads. They can be eaten as a side dish, but I like them as a substantial snack.

Put the prawns in a food processor along with a pinch each of salt and pepper. Finely chop the coriander stalks, saving the leaves to garnish the dish. Add the chopped stems to the food processor along with a third of the onions. Pulse the ingredients for a few seconds until the prawns are finely chopped but not puréed.

Transfer to a bowl and stir in the remaining onions and chopped chillies. Fry a small ball of the mixture and taste to check the seasoning. Using wet hands, roll the mixture into walnut-sized balls and coat them in the breadcrumbs.

Heat 4cm of oil in a wide pan until hot. In batches, fry the prawn koftas until golden brown all over, turning once halfway. Lift them out with a slotted spoon and drain on a plate lined with kitchen paper.

To make the sauce, heat the vegetable oil and butter in a saucepan. Add the onion, ginger and a pinch of salt and sauté for 3–4 minutes. Add the garam masala and turmeric and stir frequently for another 3–4 minutes to cook out the rawness of the spice. Pour in the coconut milk and water and bring to a simmer. Cook until the sauce has reduced by a third and thickened.

Add the prawn koftas to the pan and gently stir once to coat them in the sauce. Simmer for a few minutes until they are heated through. Transfer to a warm bowl and serve garnished with coriander leaves.

# Maharashtrian white bean patties

These little bean cakes, called *pavta* patties, are generally made with dried lima beans in India, but as these are hard to find here, use any other white bean. To save time, you can use tinned beans, but they are no match for the flavour and texture of dried ones.

Drain the beans and place in a saucepan with 1 litre of water. Bring to the boil and skim off the surface froth. Reduce the heat and simmer for 1–1½ hours until the beans are soft but not mushy. Drain well, reserving a little cooking water, and tip into a food processor. Blend to a fine purée, adding a little reserved water as necessary. Set aside.

Heat half the oil in a pan and add the mustard seeds. When they begin to pop, add the onion and seasoning. Sweat over a medium heat, stirring occasionally, for 4–6 minutes until the onion is soft. Add the turmeric, garam masala, cayenne pepper or chilli powder, ground coriander and asafoetida, if using. Fry for a few minutes until the spices are fragrant. Add the remaining oil and the potato and stir. Add a splash of water and cover the pan. Steam for 8–10 minutes over a low-to-medium heat, stirring once or twice, until the potatoes are soft. Tip in the puréed beans and chopped coriander. Lightly mash together using a potato masher. Taste and adjust the seasoning. If the mixture is too wet, add a little flour to get a fairly stiff dough. Leave to cool.

Shape the mixture into small fishcake-like patties and dust with a little flour. Heat a thin layer of oil in a wide frying pan until hot. In batches, fry the patties for 4–5 minutes until golden brown all over. Drain on kitchen paper and serve warm with a sweet-and-sour chutney.

**MAKES 8–10**

150g dried white beans (such as haricot or butter beans), soaked in water overnight
4 tbsp vegetable oil, plus extra for frying
1 tsp black mustard seeds
1 small onion, peeled and finely chopped
sea salt and freshly ground black pepper
1 tsp ground turmeric
½ tsp garam masala
½ tsp cayenne pepper (or chilli powder), to taste
1 tsp ground coriander
pinch of asafoetida (optional)
1 large potato, about 300g, peeled and diced
handful of coriander leaves, chopped
1–2 tbsp plain flour, plus extra to dust

**MAKES 12–14**
**PASTRY**
225g plain or gram flour
1½ tsp fine sea salt
1 tsp black onion seeds,
   toasted
1 tbsp vegetable oil
   (or melted unsalted
   butter), plus extra
   to brush
5–6 tbsp warm water

**FILLING**
1–2 tbsp vegetable oil
1 large onion, peeled
   and finely chopped
2 garlic cloves, peeled
   and finely chopped
2.5cm ginger, peeled
   and finely grated
1 tsp mild curry powder
¼ tsp hot chilli powder
1 tsp ground tumeric
1 tsp ground cumin
500g minced lamb
sea salt and ground
   pepper to taste
100g peas, thawed if
   frozen
1 tsp dried mango
   powder (or 1 tbsp
   fresh lemon juice)
1 mild green chilli,
   deseeded and finely
   diced
handful of mint leaves,
   chopped

# Lamb, cumin and mint samosas

These samosas are equally delicious deep-fried, which encourages their pastry casing to puff up and blister slightly. However, I have baked these in the oven as an alternative (and healthier) way of cooking them.

To make the pastry, combine the flour, salt and black onion seeds in a large bowl. Make a well in the centre and add the oil and 5 tablespoons of warm water. Mix with a butter knife to form a dough, adding more water if the mixture seems too dry. Tip onto a lightly floured work surface and knead for 5–10 minutes to a smooth dough. Cover with cling film and leave to rest in a cool place for 30 minutes.

To prepare the filling, heat the oil in a karahi or a wide pan over a medium-to-high heat. Add the onion, garlic, ginger, curry and chilli powders and ground spices. Fry for a few minutes until the onion begins to soften and the spices are fragrant. Add the lamb mince and a generous pinch each of salt and pepper. Stir-fry for 4–5 minutes until the mince is golden brown. Add the peas and dried mango powder or lemon juice and cook for a further minute before stirring in the chopped chilli and mint. Taste and adjust the seasoning, then transfer to a wide bowl and leave to cool.

Preheat the oven to 220°C/Fan 200°C/Gas 7. Divide the pastry into 6–7 equal pieces. Make each piece into a ball then roll out to a circle of about 15cm. Cut each circle into 2 equal halves. Working with one at a time, brush the cut edge of the semi-circle with a little water and form a cone shape, sealing the edge. Fill each cone with the filling up to 1cm from the top. Brush the pastry edges with water and press together to seal the cone. Place on a baking tray lined with baking parchment and repeat to make the remaining samosas. (You could also form them into teardrop shapes to make a change from the typical triangular ones.)

Brush all over each samosa with a little oil or melted butter and arrange on a lightly oiled baking tray. Bake the samosas for 14–16 minutes until golden brown and the pastry is crisp. Remove from the oven, cool for a few minutes and serve while still hot.

Lamb, cumin and mint samosas &
Mixed vegetable samosas

# Mixed vegetable samosas

**MAKES 12–14**
**PASTRY**
225g plain or gram flour,
  plus extra to dust
1½ tsp fine sea salt
1 tbsp vegetable oil,
  plus extra for
  deep-frying
5–6 tbsp warm water

Samosas come in a variety of shapes and sizes and have different names (such as *shingara* in Bengali), depending on the region or state from which they come. Some that I tried in India resembled rough, misshapened cones rather than the triangular pasties to which we are accustomed in Britain. Vegetarian samosas tend to be the most popular for light snacking, filled with any selection of vegetables and spices. If you are short of time, make these samosas using store-bought filo pastry, which will produce a lighter crust. For a golden and crisp finish, bake these with generous brushings of melted butter.

To make the pastry, combine the flour and salt in a large bowl. Make a well in the centre and add the oil and 6 tablespoons of warm water. Mix with a butter knife to form a dough, adding more water if the mixture seems too dry. Tip on to a lightly floured work surface and knead for 5–10 minutes to a smooth dough. Cover with cling film and leave to rest in a cool place for 30 minutes.

Meanwhile, prepare the filling. Heat the oil over a medium heat in a karahi or a wide pan. Sauté the onions for 3–4 minutes, stirring frequently until they soften. Cut the potato and carrot into 1cm dice, tip into the pan and fry for another 4 minutes. Add the remaining ingredients, except the fresh coriander, and season well. Stir-fry for a few minutes until the vegetables are tender and the spices no longer taste raw. Mix in the chopped coriander, transfer to a wide bowl and leave to cool completely.

Divide the pastry into 6–7 equal pieces. Make each piece into a ball then roll out to a circle of about 15cm. Cut each circle into two equal halves. Working with one at a time, brush the cut edge of the semi-circle with a little water and form a cone shape, sealing the edge. Fill each cone with the filling up to 1cm from the top. Brush the pastry edges with water and press together to seal the cone. Place on a baking tray lined with baking parchment and repeat to make the remaining samosas.

Preheat the oven to its lowest setting and heat 6cm of oil in a deep saucepan (or a deep-fryer) to 170°C. Deep-fry the samosas in batches for 4–6 minutes, turning them over halfway, until they are golden brown and crisp. Drain on a baking tray lined with kitchen paper and keep warm in the oven while you fry the rest. Serve warm.

**FILLING**
2 tbsp vegetable oil
2 medium onions, peeled and finely chopped
1 large waxy potato, about 250–300g, peeled
1 medium carrot, peeled
1 large garlic clove, peeled and finely chopped
250g mixed mushrooms, cleaned and sliced
75g peas, thawed if frozen
2 tsp ground coriander
1 tsp ground cumin
½ tsp mild chilli powder
½ tsp garam masala
pinch of caster sugar
sea salt and freshly ground black pepper
handful of coriander, finely chopped

**MAKES 12–14**

1 tsp fine sea salt

1 tsp ground turmeric

1 tsp cayenne pepper

¼ tsp freshly ground
black pepper

1 medium aubergine,
about 350g, cut in half
lengthways then into
1cm cubes

1 tbsp vegetable oil,
plus extra for
deep-frying

1 medium onion, peeled
and finely chopped

**BATTER**

150g gram (or plain)
flour

½ tsp fine sea salt

1 tsp ground turmeric

1 tsp toasted cumin
seeds

75–100ml warm water

# Aubergine bhajis

We are most familiar with onion bhajis here in the UK, and these aubergine fritters are a delicious alternative. The word *bhajia*, literally meaning 'fried', has been anglicised to the *bhaji* or *bhajee* that we recognise today. The fritters are made with a batter very similar to that used to make pakoras, but here it does not coat the main ingredient, instead the vegetable is finely chopped and mixed through the batter. You can try making the fritters with other vegetables such as courgettes, cauliflower or even okra.

First, make the batter by combining the flour, salt, turmeric and cumin seeds in a large bowl. Gradually stir in enough water to get a thick batter with a slow-dropping consistency. Leave to stand for a few minutes while you prepare the vegetables.

In a small bowl, combine the salt, turmeric, cayenne and black pepper. Sprinkle this over the aubergine and toss to coat. Heat a tablespoon of oil in a large pan and sauté the onion with a pinch of seasoning for 6–8 minutes until golden brown. Add the aubergine and cook for 3–4 minutes or until it has softened. Remove the pan from the heat and cool slightly.

Tip the aubergine and onion mixture into the batter and mix well. Preheat the oven to the lowest setting and heat 6cm of oil in a deep saucepan (or deep-fryer) to 180°C. Gently drop spoonfuls of the bhaji mixture into the hot oil and fry in batches for 4–6 minutes until evenly golden brown and crisp. Drain on a baking tray lined with kitchen paper and keep warm while you fry the rest. Serve hot and crisp with Sweet tamarind and Spicy green chutneys (see pages 217 and 215).

# Bombay potato cakes

**MAKES 10**

75g urad dal

3 medium potatoes,
about 750g, peeled and
cut into large chunks

1 tsp garam masala

juice of ½ lemon

sea salt and freshly
ground black pepper

**FILLING**

2–3 tbsp vegetable oil,
plus extra for frying

3cm ginger, peeled and
finely grated

2 green chillies,
deseeded and finely
chopped

1 tsp mild chilli powder

1 tsp cumin seeds,
roasted and ground

½ tsp ground turmeric

½ tsp ground coriander

2 tsp dried mango
powder

2 tbsp sultanas or
raisins

50g peas, thawed if
frozen

plain flour, for dusting

*Aloo tikki* or potato cakes are one of the most popular snacks in India and they are commonly sold as street snacks, cooked to order on hot portable griddles. My version includes fresh peas and urad dal (split and skinned black gram), which adds texture to the cakes.

Rinse the urad dal in several changes of cold water then soak in a bowl of water for 30 minutes. Meanwhile, boil the potatoes in a pan of well-salted water for 10–15 minutes until tender when pierced with a knife. Drain well and mash while hot with a potato ricer. Stir in the garam masala, lemon juice and seasoning to taste. Leave to cool.

Meanwhile, make the filling. Heat 2–3 tablespoons of oil in a pan. Except for the peas and flour, add all the remaining ingredients to the pan with the drained urad dal and stir-fry for 3–4 minutes until fragrant. If necessary, add a little splash of water to prevent the ingredients sticking to the base of the pan and burning. Finally, tip in the peas and season well. Stir for another couple of minutes until the peas are just cooked through. Transfer the mixture to a large bowl and leave to cool completely.

Shape large spoonfuls of the mashed potato into ten balls. Working with one at a time, flatten the ball to a circle, about 3.5cm wide, and place a teaspoonful of filling in the centre. Fold the edges together to seal in the filling, then shape into a fishcake-like patty. Dust lightly with flour then place on a plate dusted with flour. Heat a thin layer of oil in a wide non-stick frying pan. Fry the patties for 2–3 minutes each side until golden brown. (You may need to do this in several batches.) Drain on kitchen paper and serve with a Tomato and cucumber chutney or Green mango chutney (see pages 224 and 206).

# Cottage cheese and sweetcorn fritters

I am a big fan of these fritters; they are ideal starters as they have a good balance of mildly hot, sweet and savoury flavours to whet the appetite. You can use any fresh cheese in the batter. I have made these fritters with homemade paneer and even left some of the sweetcorn kernels whole for extra texture.

Put the corn kernels into a food processor and blend to a rough purée. Scrape into a bowl and set aside.

Heat the oil in a pan until hot. Add the garlic, ginger and onion and fry for 4–6 minutes, until the onion is soft and translucent. Add the puréed corn and a pinch of salt and cook for 2–3 minutes. Pour the milk into the pan and bring to a simmer. Gently stir over a medium heat and cook for 3–5 minutes until the mixture is thick and creamy.

Transfer the mixture to a large bowl and stir in the cheese, chilli, cumin, dried mango powder and coriander. Taste, and adjust the seasoning as necessary. Stir in enough flour to get an evenly combined, thick batter.

Preheat the oven to the lowest setting and heat 6cm of oil in a deep saucepan (or a deep-fryer) to 170–180°C. Carefully drop spoonfuls of the batter into the hot oil – do not overcrowd the pan as this will cause the temperature of the oil to drop. Deep-fry for 4–6 minutes, turning frequently, until golden brown all over. Drain on a baking tray lined with kitchen paper and keep warm in the oven while you fry the rest. Serve immediately while the fritters are still warm and crisp.

**MAKES 12–14**

200g fresh sweetcorn kernels (or drained tinned sweetcorn)

2 tbsp vegetable oil, plus extra for deep-frying

2 garlic cloves, peeled and finely chopped

1.5cm ginger, peeled and grated

1 small onion, peeled and finely chopped

sea salt

200ml whole milk

100g curd or cottage cheese

1 green chilli, deseeded and finely chopped

1 tsp ground cumin

1 tsp dried mango powder

2 tbsp chopped coriander

150g gram (or plain) flour

# Spicy vegetable and paneer wraps

**SERVES 4**

200g spinach leaves
2–3 tbsp vegetable oil
3cm ginger, peeled and
  finely grated
3 garlic cloves, peeled
  and finely chopped
1 green chilli, deseeded
  and finely chopped
1 small red onion,
  peeled and sliced
1 red pepper, cut into
  thin strips
2 carrots, peeled and
  cut into thin strips
1 tsp sea salt
1 tsp garam masala
1 tsp hot chilli powder
½ tsp ground cumin
225g block of paneer,
  cut into thin strips
2 tbsp chopped
  coriander
juice of ½ lemon
4 chapattis (see page
  183) or flour tortillas
Coriander and chilli
  raita (see page 202)

Vegetable wraps are typical street foods in India, particularly in busy cities like Calcutta where the notion of grabbing a cheap, nutritious, convenient snack is always appealing. If you prefer a non-vegetarian version or a more substantial filling, add cooked mince or spicy chicken pieces. This would also make a lovely lunch with a fresh and zingy salad.

Bring a pan of salted water to the boil. Add the spinach and blanch for 30 seconds to 1 minute until wilted. Drain well and set aside.

Heat the oil in a large frying pan over a medium heat. Add the ginger, garlic, chilli and onion and cook for 2–3 minutes, stirring frequently. Add the red pepper and carrots and stir well. After a few minutes, add the salt, garam masala, chilli powder and cumin. Continue to fry until the vegetables have slightly softened yet still retain some bite. Lastly, stir through the strips of paneer, chopped coriander and lemon juice and cook for a few minutes. Remove the pan from the hob.

Warm the chapattis in a wide, dry frying pan to soften them a little. (This makes them easier to wrap with.) Spread a tablespoon of Coriander and chilli raita on each warmed chapatti and cover with a layer of blanched spinach. Spoon the vegetable and paneer filling on top and roll up the chapatti to enclose the filling, as you would a parcel.

Wrap each spicy vegetable wrap in baking parchment and foil (or old newspaper) and serve warm. If you find the wraps have gone cold, warm them through in a hot oven for a few minutes before serving.

# Aloo dahi puri

These little crispy filled puris are what I consider to be the ultimate *chaat* – a Hindi word that describes the various savoury delicacies that tempt passers-by to the roadside food carts found in every Indian city. You will need to make a trip to your nearest Indian grocer to secure a box of ready-made mini *pani puri* shells and a bag of *sev mamra* (crispy snacks consisting of a mixture of puffed rice, fried yellow gram noodles and spiced peanuts). Thereafter, it will only take minutes to assemble these delicious bite-sized treats.

First, prepare the potato filling. Peel and cut the potato into large chunks then boil in a pan of salted water for 10–15 minutes until tender. Drain well, then chop the potato into a small dice. Place in a bowl and mix with the chilli powder, cumin, garam masala, dried mango powder, onion, yoghurt and seasoning to taste.

When you are about ready to eat, carefully break the top of each puri to make a small hole that is big enough to add the potato filling through. (The puris are very delicate so you do need to be gentle with them.) Fill each puri with some potato mixture and a drizzle each of yoghurt and tamarind chutney. Garnish with the chopped coriander and sev mamra or sev. Serve immediately.

**SERVES 4**

12 ready-made pani puri shells (also known as *golgappa*)
150ml natural yoghurt
6–8 tbsp Sweet tamarind chutney (see page 217)
handful of coriander, leaves chopped, and handful of *sev mamra* (or plain sev), to garnish

**POTATO FILLING**

1 large waxy potato, about 250–300g
½ tsp red chilli powder
¼ tsp ground cumin
¼ tsp garam masala
½ tsp dried mango powder
1 small onion, peeled and finely diced
200ml natural yoghurt, mixed with 2–3 tbsp water
fine sea salt and freshly ground black pepper

# Fish

Bengali prawn curry

Hyderabadi squid tamatar

Spiced fish wrapped in banana leaves

Fish tenga

Baked whole sea bass with green masala paste

Majuli fishcakes with tomato relish

Monkfish moilee

Tuna vattichathu

Goan fish ambotik

Dry crab curry

Grilled snapper with dry spices

Crispy battered fish with spiced okra and aubergine

Mackerel masala

Pan-fried John Dory with hot-spiced red curry sauce

# Bengali prawn curry

SERVES 4

400g large raw prawns,
  shell on
½ tsp ground turmeric
sea salt
2 onions, peeled and
  roughly chopped
2cm ginger, peeled and
  roughly chopped
3 garlic cloves, peeled
  and roughly chopped
2 green chillies,
  deseeded and chopped
2 tbsp vegetable oil
2 tsp mustard seeds
½ tsp hot chilli powder
2 whole cloves
4 green cardamom pods
1 cinnamon stick
2 bay leaves
1 whole dried chilli
400ml tin coconut milk

This prawn curry is considered a classic dish, and marinating seafood or meat with a combination of salt and turmeric is characteristic of Bengali cooking. I love how the complementary sweetness of the prawns and coconut is contrasted with the heat and pungency of the chillies and mustard seeds. Needless to say, very fresh prawns are essential for this recipe.

Shell and devein the prawns, leaving the tails on, if you wish. Place them in a bowl with the turmeric and a pinch of salt. Mix well, then leave to marinate for 5–10 minutes. Meanwhile, put the onions, ginger, garlic and chillies into a food processor with 2 tablespoons of water. Blend to a fine wet paste.

Heat the oil in a large pan. Add the mustard seeds, chilli powder, cloves, cardamom, cinnamon, bay leaves and whole chilli. Fry for 1–2 minutes until the spices become fragrant and the mustard seeds begin to sputter. Add the wet paste to the pan and fry over a low heat for 12–15 minutes, stirring frequently.

Add the coconut milk to the pan and bring to a simmer over a low heat. Add the prawns and simmer for 2–3 minutes, until they are opaque and just cooked through. Transfer to a warm bowl and serve immediately with warm Indian breads or rice.

# Hyderabadi squid tamatar

**SERVES 4**

700g baby squid, cleaned
3 garlic cloves, peeled and chopped
2.5cm ginger, peeled and chopped
1 small onion, peeled and roughly chopped
2 tbsp vegetable oil
2 tbsp malt or cider vinegar
1 tsp ground cumin
1 tsp ground turmeric
6 black peppercorns, freshly crushed
1 tsp sea salt, or to taste
¼ tsp ground nutmeg
¼ tsp ground cloves
400g ripe plum tomatoes, skinned and chopped
1 cinnamon stick
2 bay leaves
freshly ground black pepper

Hyderabad, the capital of Andhra Pradesh, has a 400-year-old culinary history, which has produced a cuisine that is a blend of Moghlai and Persian cooking. Tomatoes (*tamatar*) and black peppercorns feature largely in Hyderabadi cuisine. Both of these ingredients combine to create a delectable blend of flavours in this dish. The mouth-watering sauce also works well with fresh prawns, crayfish or meaty chunks of monkfish.

Pull out the tentacles from the main body of the squids then cut the body into halves. Set aside.

Put the garlic, ginger and onion in a food processor and blend to fine wet paste. If necessary, add a tablespoon of water to get an even blend. Heat the oil in a large pan over a medium heat and, when hot, add the wet paste. Cook for about 15–20 minutes, stirring frequently to prevent it catching and burning. When the onion paste is golden brown, add the vinegar and cook until the liquid has evaporated. Add the cumin, turmeric, crushed peppercorns, salt, nutmeg and cloves and gently fry for 2 minutes to allow the spices to cook out.

Add the tomatoes, cinnamon, bay leaves and 150ml water. Cover and simmer for about 45 minutes. Add the squid, stir and gently simmer, uncovered, for 5 minutes, until it is just cooked through and tender.

Ladle into a warm serving bowl, grind over a little black pepper and serve immediately.

# Spiced fish wrapped in banana leaves

**SERVES 4**
1 whole tilapia, about 800–900g, cleaned and gutted (or 4 kingfish steaks weighing about 150–170g each)
1 tsp mild chilli powder
½ tsp ground turmeric
juice of ½ lime
sea salt and freshly ground black pepper
2 banana leaves, washed

**SPICE PASTE**
4 tbsp vegetable oil
2 small onions, peeled and finely chopped
1 large garlic clove, peeled and finely crushed
2cm ginger, peeled and finely grated
1 green chilli, deseeded and finely chopped
4 curry leaves, roughly chopped
6 plum tomatoes, chopped
¼ tsp ground turmeric
1 tsp lime juice

This dish is the Keralan delicacy *karimeen pollichathu*, essentially a spiced fish wrapped in a banana leaf, which is cooked in a hot pan so that the leaves char slightly and the fish inside acquires a mild smoky flavour.

Karimeen (also known as pearl spot) is a sustainable fish that is abundant in the backwaters of Kerala, where the freshwater of the river converges with the saltwater from the sea. To me, it has a delicate flesh that tastes sweeter than a Dover sole. You could substitute it with tilapia, snapper, kingfish, John Dory or any other firm flat fish. Here's a very good tip from Thressi John Kottukapally, the chef who first cooked the dish for me: first warm the banana leaves over a low flame so that they become pliable and easy to wrap around the fish.

Wash and pat dry the fish with kitchen paper. Score the flesh on both sides of the whole fish. (This is not necessary if you're using kingfish steaks.)

In a small bowl, mix together the chilli powder, turmeric, lime juice and ⅓ teaspoon each of salt and pepper. Rub this all over the fish, including the gut cavity. Cover the fish with cling film and leave to marinate while you prepare the spice paste.

Heat 2 tablespoons of oil in a large frying pan, add the onions, garlic, ginger, chilli and curry leaves and sauté gently for 4–5 minutes until the onions begin to soften. Stir in the tomatoes, turmeric and lime juice and season well with salt and pepper. Cook for a further 3–5 minutes over a medium heat until the tomatoes are soft and the mixture is thick and resembles a sticky paste. Leave to cool.

Hold the banana leaves over a low flame on the hob to soften them slightly. Overlap the leaves on the work surface, shiny side up. Spoon a little spice paste on to the middle of the leaves, place the fish on top, then spoon over the remaining spice paste. Wrap the leaves around the fish, like a parcel, and secure the ends with cocktail sticks. (If using kingfish steaks, wrap each steak individually with smaller pieces of banana leaf.)

Place a large non-stick pan or wok (with a lid) over a moderate heat and add the remaining oil, swirling to coat. Carefully lower the wrapped fish into the pan and cover it with the lid. Cook for 15–20 minutes, gently turning over halfway through. When done, the banana leaves will brown and char slightly. (Individually wrapped kingfish steaks may take less time – about 10–15 minutes.)

Transfer the parcel to a warm serving plate and bring to the table. Open it up to release the wonderful aromas and enjoy with steamed basmati rice.

4 salmon or kingfish
  steaks, about
  125–150g each
sea salt and freshly
  ground black pepper
3 tbsp mustard oil
small bunch coriander,
  stems and leaves
  roughly chopped, plus
  extra leaves to garnish
2 green chillies,
  deseeded and chopped
3cm ginger, peeled and
  chopped
5–6 garlic cloves, peeled
  and chopped
1 tsp ground turmeric
200ml water
1 large waxy potato,
  about 300g, peeled and
  diced
4 tomatoes, deseeded
  and roughly chopped
pinch of caster sugar
  (optional)

# Fish tenga

This is a light and sour fish curry that is typical in Assam, a state in northeast India. The dish derives its name from the elephant apples (*outenga* in Assamese) that are used to impart a sharp, astringent flavour. Elephant apples are specific to the region and are seasonal, available mostly during the autumn months; so for this reason tenga recipes may include other souring agents such as lemon juice, mangosteen or, in this case, tomatoes. This particular recipe has been adapted from the dish cooked for me by Atul Lahkar, a chef and restaurateur in Majuli who showed me that it is possible to cook a delicious meal with very basic resources.

Rub the fish steaks all over with a little salt and pepper. Heat half the oil in a wide, non-stick frying pan and add the fish steaks when hot. Fry for about 2 minutes on each side until golden brown and just cooked through. Remove to a plate and set aside.

Put the coriander, chillies, ginger and garlic into a food processor and blend to a fine wet paste. Heat the remaining oil in a wide pan and add the blended paste and turmeric. Fry for a few minutes until fragrant, then tip in the water. Bring to a simmer then add the potato, tomatoes and seasoning to taste. Cook gently for about 10–15 minutes until the tomatoes have broken down and the potato is tender. Taste and adjust the seasoning with a pinch of sugar, if you prefer.

Add the fish steaks to the pan and gently heat in the sauce until warmed through. Sprinkle the curry with a few coriander leaves and serve immediately with steamed basmati rice.

# Baked whole sea bass with green masala paste

This easy recipe is fairly versatile. You can either follow my suggestion and oven steam the fish in the banana leaves, or simply bake it unwrapped on a lightly oiled baking tray. Either method produces a lovely dish that needs only some rice and a relish to accompany it.

First, make the green masala paste. Put all the ingredients into a food processor and blend well to a smooth paste. Preheat the oven to 180°C/Fan 160°C/Gas 4.

Slightly overlap the banana leaves on a large, lipped baking tray. Wash the cavity of the fish, pat dry and score the flesh on both sides. Spread the masala paste along both lengths of the fish, including the gut cavity, and place the fish on the banana leaves. Arrange the thin slices of lime on top of the fish. Wrap the fish with the banana leaves and secure the ends with cocktail sticks.

Bake in the preheated oven for 30–35 minutes until the fish is just cooked through. Open up the parcel at the table and serve at once with some plain steamed rice or Coconut rice (see page 169).

**SERVES 4–6**
2 large banana leaves
1 whole sea bass, about
 1.5–1.8kg, scaled and
 gutted
1 lime, cut into thin
 slices

**GREEN MASALA PASTE**
100g mint leaves,
 roughly chopped
100g coriander leaves,
 roughly chopped
3 garlic cloves, peeled
 and roughly chopped
2.5cm ginger, peeled
 and roughly chopped
2–3 green chillies,
 deseeded and chopped
1–2 tbsp garam masala
1 tsp sea salt
1 tsp caster sugar
1 tbsp lime juice
2 tbsp water
2 tbsp vegetable oil

400g firm white fish
  fillets
2.5cm ginger, peeled
  and finely grated
sea salt and freshly
  ground black pepper
mustard or vegetable
  oil, for frying
1 large floury potato,
  about 250g, peeled
2 red chillies
½ tsp ground turmeric
2 garlic cloves, peeled
  and finely crushed
1 tsp ground cumin
1 tsp ground coriander
handful of coriander
  leaves
2 medium egg yolks
2 medium eggs
2–3 tbsp plain flour
50g dried breadcrumbs

# Majuli fishcakes with tomato relish

I first made these fishcakes in Majuli, the largest freshwater island on the Brahmaputra river, situated in the state of Assam. Out there, it was pure back-to-basics cooking and we used whatever ingredients were available locally. The fish we managed to catch that day happened to be a rohu, a freshwater fish from the carp family with a mildly sweet flesh. However, any firm white fish or even picked crab-meat will work for this recipe. I have also adapted the dish to include some ground spice and a crisp breadcrumb coating.

Pat dry the fish fillets then rub them all over with the ginger and some salt and pepper. Heat a thin layer of oil in a wide frying pan until hot. Add the fish and fry for about 1½ minutes on each side until just cooked through. Remove to a plate and leave to cool.

Meanwhile, cut the potato into large chunks and add it to a pan with the whole chillies and turmeric, then fill with enough water to cover. Bring to a gentle boil and cook the potato for 10–15 minutes until tender. Drain well and discard the chillies. While still hot, mash the potato using a potato ricer into a large bowl. Leave to cool slightly, then stir in the garlic, cumin and ground coriander. Chop the fresh coriander and add it to the mixture with seasoning to taste. Flake the fish and add to the potato along with the egg yolks. Mix well and chill for at least 30 minutes to firm up slightly.

To make the tomato relish, gently sauté the onion and garlic in the oil with some salt and pepper for 5–6 minutes until soft and translucent. Tip into a bowl. Deseed and chop the tomatoes and add to the bowl with the lime juice and a pinch of sugar to taste. Set aside.

With damp hands, mould the fish and potato mixture into 12 patties. Beat the eggs and coat the fishcakes in the flour, beaten egg and breadcrumbs. Heat a thin layer of oil in a wide frying pan and fry the patties in several batches. Cook for 2–3 minutes on each side over a moderate heat until golden brown. Drain on a plate lined with kitchen paper, then sprinkle over a little salt. Keep warm in a low oven while you fry the rest.

Divide the fishcakes among warm plates and serve while still hot with the tomato relish alongside.

**TOMATO RELISH**
1 large onion, peeled
  and finely chopped
2 garlic cloves, peeled
  and finely crushed
1½ tbsp vegetable oil
3 plum tomatoes
juice of 1 lime
pinch of caster sugar

# Monkfish moilee

**SERVES 4**

500g skinless and
  boneless monkfish
  tails
¼ tsp ground turmeric
½ tsp sea salt, or to taste
juice of 1 lime
2 tbsp vegetable oil
1 large onion, peeled
  and finely chopped
3cm ginger, peeled and
  finely grated
3 garlic cloves, peeled
  and finely crushed
3 green chillies,
  deseeded and slice
  in half lengthways
4 curry leaves
½ tsp sea salt
400ml tin coconut milk
6 cherry tomatoes,
  quartered
handful of coriander
  leaves, to garnish

*Meen* or fish moilee is a simple coconut fish curry from Kerala on the west coast of India. Some consider it an Anglo–Indian dish as it was commonly found in other Southeast Asian cuisines connected through the British empire. Meaty and robust monkfish tails are ideal for this curry, but you can also choose to use more delicate sea bass or haddock fillets. If using the latter, try not to stir the curry too much to prevent the fish breaking up during cooking.

Cut the monkfish tails into bite-sized chunks and place in a bowl. Mix together the turmeric, salt and lime juice to create a wet paste then mix this with the monkfish chunks and leave to marinate for about 20 minutes.

Heat the oil in a large heavy-based pan over a medium-to-high heat. Add the onion, ginger, garlic, chillies, curry leaves and salt. Stir frequently for 5–6 minutes until the onion is translucent and soft. Pour in the coconut milk and bring to a gentle simmer, stirring occasionally. Add the marinated fish and cherry tomatoes. Gently simmer for another 4–5 minutes until the fish is cooked through.

Ladle the curry into a warm serving bowl and garnish with coriander leaves. Serve with plain basmati rice.

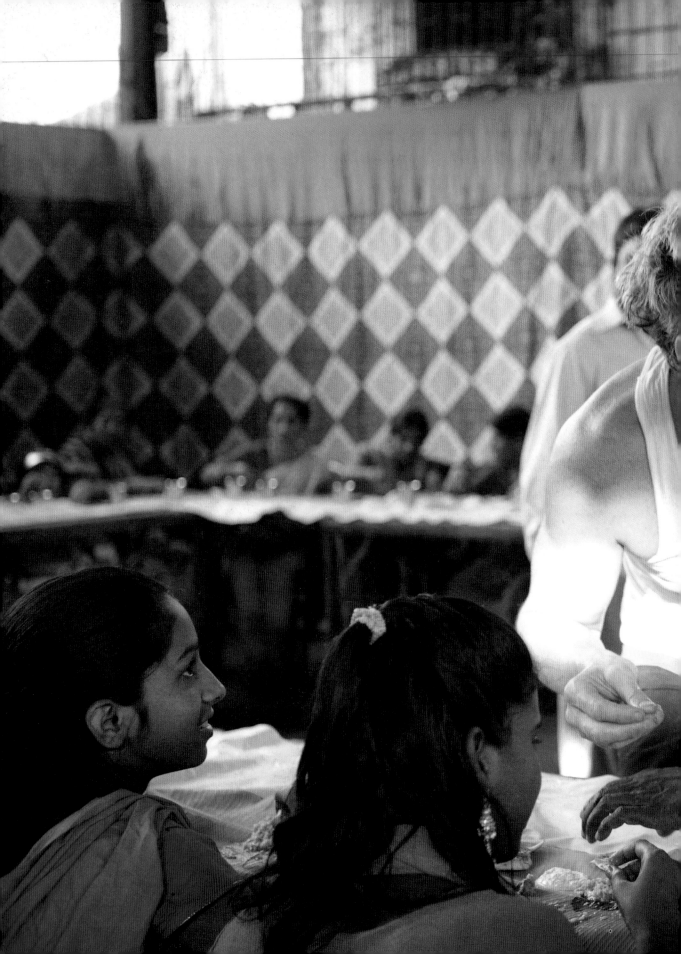

# Tuna vattichathu

**SERVES 4**

500g tuna steaks
sea salt and freshly
 ground black pepper
3 tbsp coconut or
 vegetable oil
3 garlic cloves, peeled
 and finely chopped
3cm ginger, peeled and
 finely shredded into
 matchsticks
1 tsp hot chilli powder
½ tsp ground turmeric
½ tsp fenugreek
2–3 tsp tamarind paste,
 to taste
150g finely grated
 coconut (optional)
1 red chilli, halved
 lengthways, with seeds
 removed if you prefer
200ml water
6–8 curry leaves
1 tsp black mustard
 seeds

This is another popular fish dish from Kerala. The curry is usually cooked with oily fish such as sardines and mackerel in an earthenware pot called a *chatty*. For a less greasy finish I'm using fresh tuna, which tastes fantastic in the hot and spicy sauce. Traditionally, *kokum* (made from dried mangosteen peel) is used as a souring agent for this dish, but as it is difficult to source in the UK I'm using tamarind paste instead.

Cut the tuna into bite-sized pieces and mix with a little salt and pepper. Set aside.

Heat 2 tablespoons of oil in a wide pan and fry the garlic, ginger, chilli powder, turmeric and fenugreek. Stir-fry for a few minutes until the paste is fragrant. Add the tamarind paste, grated coconut, if using, and red chilli and stir-fry for a couple more minutes.

Pour in the water and bring to a gentle simmer. Add the tuna to the pan and stir well to coat in the sauce. Simmer gently for 3–4 minutes until the fish is just cooked through. Taste, adjust the seasoning, then transfer the curry to a warm serving bowl.

Heat the remaining oil in a small saucepan and fry the curry leaves and mustard seeds over a medium heat for 1–2 minutes until fragrant and the mustard seeds begin to sputter. Tip the curry leaves, seeds and oil over the curry and give it one or two stirs. Serve immediately with steamed rice or warm Indian breads.

# Goan fish ambotik

This sour and fiery fish curry comes from Goa, and it is popular among the Catholics in the region. It is widely thought that the dish has Portuguese–Indian origins, because *ambot* indicates 'sour' and *tik* means 'spicy' in Portuguese. This is also exemplified by the typical Portuguese practice of using vinegar in cooking. The curry is commonly made with shark or skate caught along the western Indian coastline, but use any firm-fleshed fish, such as kingfish, monkfish, halibut or tuna, or even an oily fish like mackerel, cut across the bone into steaks.

Cut the fish into bite-sized chunks and place in a large bowl with the tamarind paste and a little seasoning. Mix well and set aside to marinate while you prepare the rest of the dish.

To make the hot and sour chilli paste, place all the ingredients in a food processor and blend to a fine wet paste. If necessary, add a tablespoon or two of water and scrape down the sides of the bowl a few times to get the paste evenly ground.

Heat the oil in a wide pan and add the onion and some seasoning. Stir frequently over a medium-to-high heat for 6–8 minutes until the onion is translucent, soft and lightly browned. Tip in the chilli paste and fry for another couple of minutes until fragrant. Add the fish pieces to the pan and stir gently to coat in the sauce. If the sauce seems too dry, add a splash of water. Simmer for 3–4 minutes until the fish is just cooked through. Taste and adjust the seasoning. Serve garnished with some coriander leaves and plenty of plain basmati rice.

**SERVES 4**

500g firm-fleshed fish (see intro left)
1½ tbsp tamarind paste
sea salt and freshly ground black pepper
1 tbsp vegetable oil
1 large onion, peeled and finely chopped
handful of coriander leaves, to garnish

**HOT AND SOUR CHILLI PASTE**

6 red chillies, deseeded and roughly chopped
1 tsp cumin seeds
½ tsp black peppercorns
2.5cm ginger, peeled and chopped
3 garlic cloves, peeled and chopped
2 tsp malt or cider vinegar
1 tsp caster sugar

# Dry crab curry

**SERVES 4**

1kg cooked crab claws,
  thawed if frozen
3 tbsp vegetable oil
½ tsp fenugreek,
  crushed with a pinch
  of salt
1 tsp fennel seeds
6 curry leaves
2.5cm ginger, peeled
  and finely grated
6 garlic cloves, peeled
  and finely chopped
4 onions, peeled and
  finely chopped
1 tsp hot chilli powder
2 tsp ground coriander
1½ tsp ground turmeric
½ tsp sea salt, or to taste
4 tomatoes, peeled and
  roughly chopped
100g grated coconut

I am partial to cooking crab on the shell because I find that food tastes especially delicious when you're forced to use your fingers and 'work' for little bites of pleasure. This curry only requires half the effort as it is far easier to extract the flesh from meaty crab claws rather than from the body of whole small crabs, which is what they would use in India. Enjoy the curry with some plain steamed rice.

Crack the crab claws by tapping them with the back of a strong cleaver, heavy pestle or rolling pin. Set aside.

Heat the oil in a large pan or wok and fry the fenugreek, fennel seeds and curry leaves for 1–2 minutes until they become very aromatic. Add the ginger, garlic and onions and fry for 6–8 minutes, stirring occasionally, until the onions have softened and lightly browned. If the mixture starts to stick to the bottom of the pan, add a little splash of water.

Add the chilli powder, coriander, turmeric and salt to the pan and stir well. After a minute or two, add the chopped tomatoes. Continue to fry until most of the liquid has been cooked off and the pan is quite dry. Stir in the crab claws and leave to simmer for 4–6 minutes, until heated through.

Meanwhile, dry-roast the grated coconut in a hot pan for 3–4 minutes or until it turns golden brown. Sprinkle the toasted coconut on top of the curry and stir well. Transfer to a warm bowl and serve immediately.

# Grilled snapper with dry spices

This is one of the easiest and quickest ways to cook fish, using what I would consider storecupboard ingredients. The dry spice paste is wonderfully aromatic and really enhances the flavour of the fish.

First, make the dry spice paste. Place a frying pan over a medium heat and carefully roast the coriander, fennel and cumin seeds. Tip into a small bowl and add the garlic powder, salt, sugar and paprika. Stir in the lemon juice and vegetable oil and whisk together until well combined.

Preheat the grill to the highest setting. Rub the dry spice paste all over the snapper fillets then place on a lightly oiled baking tray, skin-side up. Cook the fish under the hot grill for about 5 minutes until firm and just cooked through. Serve immediately with some lime wedges to squeeze over.

**SERVES 4**

4 red snapper fillets,
   each about 150–170g
lime wedges, to serve

**DRY SPICE PASTE**

2 tsp coriander seeds
2 tsp fennel seeds
1 tsp cumin seeds
1 tsp garlic powder
1 tsp sea salt
2 tsp caster sugar
2 tsp ground paprika
1–2 tbsp lemon juice,
   to taste
1½ tbsp vegetable oil

# Crispy battered fish with spiced okra and aubergine

**SERVES 4**

4 Dover sole fillets, about 150g each
30g rice (or plain) flour
½ tsp ground turmeric
sea salt and freshly ground black pepper
vegetable oil, for deep-frying

**FISH BATTER**

100g plain flour
100g rice flour
generous pinch of sea salt
½ tsp baking powder
300ml cold beer
2 large egg whites

This is not an authentic Indian dish but one I created as part of a recipe challenge. It features *karimeen*, which is a fantastic fish that is unfortunately unavailable for British consumption. As this recipe is very loosely based on our much loved battered fish back home (without the chips!) you can use any white fish that you might find on offer at your local fishmonger. I've chosen Dover sole here, for its silky smooth and delicate flesh, but a less expensive variety of the sole family would work just as well.

Pat the fish fillets dry with kitchen paper, then trim the fillets to about 8–10cm each. Mix together the flour and turmeric and season with a pinch each of salt and pepper. Lightly dust the fish fillets in the flour mixture and shake off any excess.

To make the batter, sift the flours, salt and baking powder together in a large bowl. Whisk in enough beer to make a loose batter. In a separate bowl, whisk the egg whites together until they form stiff peaks. Fold the egg whites into the batter to combine, adding any extra beer if necessary to loosen the mixture. Set aside.

Heat the oil in a deep-fat fryer to 180–190°C. Deep-fry the okra in the hot oil, in batches, for 2–3 minutes. Remove and drain on kitchen paper. Once cool enough to handle, cut the okra into approximately 1.5cm pieces. Deep-fry the aubergine in batches for 1–2 minutes. Remove and drain well on kitchen paper. Set aside. Reserve the oil.

Meanwhile, heat the coconut or vegetable oil in a large pan and sauté the shallots with the cumin seeds, cinnamon, star anise, cloves, turmeric and a pinch each of salt and pepper. Sauté for a few minutes until the shallots have softened. Add the okra and aubergine to the pan and continue to cook for another 4–5 minutes, stirring frequently until the mixture has softened. Stir in the coriander and check the seasoning. If necessary, drain the mixture through a sieve placed over a bowl to drain away any excess oil. Remove the star anise and discard. Keep warm.

To fry the fish, dip each fillet into the batter and then lower into the reserved hot oil. Cook in batches for 2–3 minutes or until golden brown. Drain on kitchen paper.

Put neat dessertspoonfuls of the spiced okra and aubergine mixture on each warm serving plate. Top with the crispy battered fish and serve at once.

## SPICED OKRA AND AUBERGINE

200g okra, trimmed
1 large aubergine, diced into 1.5cm pieces
2 tbsp coconut or vegetable oil
3 shallots, peeled and finely sliced
2 tsp cumin seeds, toasted
1 tsp ground cinnamon
1 star anise
¼ tsp ground cloves
¼ tsp ground turmeric
handful of coriander, leaves chopped

Mackerel masala

**SERVES 4**

500g mackerel, cleaned
and gutted
½ tsp ground turmeric
sea salt and freshly
ground black pepper
2 tbsp vegetable oil
1 onion, peeled and
finely chopped
4 tomatoes, skinned
and finely chopped
½ tbsp tomato purée
handful of coriander
leaves, to garnish

**MASALA PASTE**

2 tsp ground coriander
½ tsp ground turmeric
1 tbsp mild chilli
powder
½ cinnamon stick
3 green cardamom
pods, seeds removed
3 whole cloves
1 bay leaf
2cm ginger, peeled and
roughly chopped
4 garlic cloves, peeled
and roughly chopped
2 large onions, peeled
and roughly chopped
2 tbsp malt vinegar
2 tbsp granulated sugar

# Mackerel masala

Mackerel is commonly found in India and is particularly popular in the south, where it is often cooked with a sweet and sour masala. While our British mackerel tends to be slightly slimmer, it has a very similar flavour and texture and is ideal for this dish. As the oily flesh of the mackerel degrades quickly, it is imperative that you use only the freshest fish. Cutting fish across the bone into small steaks is standard practice in India, as you get more flavour out of the bones and the fish is less likely to break into pieces during cooking. However, feel free to fillet and debone the mackerel to make it easier to eat.

Cut the mackerel across the bone into 2–2.5cm thick steaks and discard the heads. Rub all over with a little turmeric, salt and pepper. Make the masala paste by blending all the ingredients to a fine paste using a food processor, stopping and scraping the sides of the bowl as necessary.

Heat the oil in a large frying pan, add the onion and some seasoning and sauté for 6–8 minutes until soft and lightly golden. Scrape the masala paste into the pan and allow the spices to cook out for 3–4 minutes, stirring frequently to prevent the masala from catching and burning.

Stir in the chopped tomatoes and tomato purée. After 3–4 minutes place the mackerel pieces in the pan and increase the heat slightly. Cook for 3–4 minutes or until the mackerel is just cooked through and the sauce is quite thick. Scatter with the coriander leaves and serve straight away.

# Pan-fried John Dory with hot-spiced red curry sauce

This is another recipe I developed for my karimeen recipe challenge. Of course, I have to substitute karimeen with John Dory, which suits me perfectly as I love its sweet flavour. This dish is quite elegant and would be perfect for a dinner-party main course, particularly as the sauce can be made in advance and reheated just before you fry the fish fillets.

Heat half the oil in a large pan and, once hot, add the mustard seeds. When they sputter, add the fenugreek and cook for 30 seconds. Stir in the shallots, ginger, garlic, chillies and curry leaves and sauté for 4–5 minutes until softened. Add the chilli powder and cook for 1 minute. Stir in the tomato purée and cook for 2–3 minutes.

Add the tamarind paste followed by the coconut milk. Bring to the boil and then simmer gently for 15–20 minutes. Taste and adjust the seasoning, then transfer the sauce to a food processor and blend until smooth. Pass through a fine sieve, then return to the pan to reheat.

For the fish, heat the remaining oil in a wide, non-stick frying pan. Season the fillets and fry, skin-side down, for 1–2 minutes until the skin is crisp and the fish is cooked two-thirds through. Flip them over and cook the flesh side for 30 seconds. Remove from the heat.

Spoon the red curry sauce on to a large, shallow serving bowl and arrange the pan-fried John Dory fillets on top. Serve immediately with warm Indian breads or rice.

**SERVES 4**

4 tbsp coconut or vegetable oil
2 tsp black mustard seeds
2 tsp fenugreek
4 shallots, peeled and thinly sliced
3cm ginger, peeled and finely chopped
4 garlic cloves, peeled and finely chopped
2 green chillies, deseeded and finely chopped
8 curry leaves
2 tsp hot chilli powder
2 tbsp tomato purée
2–3 tbsp tamarind paste
400ml tin coconut milk
sea salt and freshly ground black pepper
4 John Dory fillets, about 150g each, pin bones removed

# Poultry & meat

Chilli beef fry

Chicken palak

Lamb korma

Spiced pan-fried chicken with pumpkin purée

Punjabi masala chops

Butter chicken

Guinea fowl in tomato and coconut curry

Chicken badami

Malabar duck

Spiced leg of lamb wrapped with spring onions

Tribal chicken casserole with tamarind

Quail tandoori

Chicken and papaya curry

Venison stew

# Chilli beef fry

This is my version of the chilli beef fry I sampled in one of the many toddy shops along the Kerala coast. A toddy shop is a scaled-down Indian equivalent of our local pub, and a toddy is a potent drink made from the fermented sap of a palm or coconut tree. It packs a mean punch due to the high alcohol content. There is little doubt in my mind that the hot, spicy and salty chilli beef fry is served to encourage more drinking from the punters. I've toned down the dish slightly to make it a little more balanced and omitted the toddy, which is difficult to find here, to say the least. Serve it with plain rice, a side vegetable, some cooling raita and a sweet chutney.

**SERVES 4**
600g beef fillet
1 tsp hot chilli powder
pinch of chilli flakes
1 tsp dried mango
  powder
3cm ginger, peeled and
  grated
sea salt and freshly
  ground black pepper
1 tsp coconut oil
  (optional)
vegetable oil, for
  deep-frying
1 large onion, peeled
  and very finely
  chopped
2 dried red chillies
1 tsp caster sugar
juice of 2 limes
3 tbsp rice or corn flour
1 fresh red chilli,
  deseeded and thinly
  sliced

Cut the beef into thin strips and put it into a large dish with half the chilli powder, the chilli flakes, dried mango powder, ginger and some seasoning. Add the coconut oil, if using, and mix well. Let the meat marinate for 15–20 minutes before cooking.

Heat a tablespoon of oil in a pan and add the onion, chillies, remaining chilli powder and a pinch of salt. Cook, stirring every now and then, for 5–6 minutes until the onion is soft and translucent. Add the sugar and fry for a few more minutes until the onion begins to caramelise. Add the lime juice and take the pan off the heat.

Heat 5cm of oil in a deep pan until hot. Toss the beef in the flour until evenly coated then deep-fry in batches for 2–3 minutes until brown and crisp. Drain on a plate lined with kitchen paper. When all the beef has been cooked, toss the strips with the onion mixture and sliced chilli. Transfer to a warm plate and serve immediately.

# Chicken palak

**SERVES 4**

500g boneless and
  skinless chicken
  thighs
sea salt and freshly
  ground black pepper
400g spinach leaves
2 tbsp ghee or melted
  unsalted butter
2 bay leaves
3 cloves
6–8 black peppercorns
1 cinnamon stick
1 tsp cumin seeds
1 large onion, peeled
  and thinly sliced
2 garlic cloves, peeled
  and grated
2cm ginger, peeled and
  grated
2 green chillies,
  deseeded and finely
  chopped
1 tsp mild chilli powder
½ tsp ground turmeric
1 tsp ground coriander
2 large tomatoes,
  skinned and chopped
½ tsp garam masala

This mildly spiced curry is a great introduction to Indian food. It's a healthy dish, and with a sauce made from spinach it's a great way to get kids to eat their greens, though you may want to adjust the amount of chillies and chilli powder used accordingly. I like to brown the butter for the sauce to create a nutty flavour to complement the earthy spinach. I've also chopped half the blanched spinach to give the dish a varied texture, but you may wish to purée the whole lot to stop fussy young children picking it out.

Cut the chicken into bite-sized pieces and mix with a pinch each of salt and pepper. Set aside.

Bring a large pan of salted water to the boil, add the spinach and blanch for 2–3 minutes. Drain well. Tip half of the spinach into a food processor and blend to a smooth purée. Finely chop the remaining spinach and set aside.

Place a large non-stick pan over a low heat, add the ghee or butter and cook until it turns a light brown colour, but do not let it burn. Add the bay leaves, cloves, black peppercorns, cinnamon and cumin seeds. Fry for a minute or until the spices become very aromatic.

Add the sliced onion and increase the heat to medium. Continue to fry, stirring occasionally, for 6–8 minutes until the onion is a light golden brown. Add the garlic, ginger and green chillies to the pan and fry for 2 minutes before stirring in the chilli powder, turmeric and coriander. Fry for a further 30 seconds and then stir in the chopped tomatoes. Continue to cook for 10–12 minutes until the oil begins to separate from the sauce.

Add the chicken pieces and mix well. Cook for 5 minutes then reduce the heat and partially cover the pan with a lid. Simmer gently for 30 minutes until the chicken is tender, adding a little water to the pan if it seems too dry.

Add the puréed and chopped spinach and the garam masala to the pan and stir well. Re-cover and cook for 10 more minutes. Serve hot with warm Indian flatbreads or basmati rice.

# Lamb korma

Korma recipes can be traced back to the sixteenth century. My modern lamb version is mildly spiced and creamy, quite different from your average take-away, which I often find to be overly sweet. Wherever we went in India, this dish would be called mutton korma and the meat used could either be goat or lamb. You can achieve delicious results using either meat, but if you use goat, get a young, tender one.

Cut the lamb into 3cm pieces and set aside. Put the chillies, almonds, cashews, garlic, ginger and water in a food processor and blend to a fine wet paste, scraping down the sides of the bowl. Set aside.

Heat half the oil in a heavy-based pan until hot. Season the lamb pieces and fry in batches for about 2 minutes on each side until browned all over. Transfer each batch to a plate as they are browned. Add the remaining oil to the pan and tip in the cinnamon, cloves, bay leaf, coriander and cardamom. Stir-fry for a minute until fragrant. Add the onions and some seasoning. Cook, stirring occasionally, for 5–6 minutes until the onions are soft and lightly golden.

Mix the yoghurt with the wet nut paste and the saffron water, then add to the pan, stirring well. Cook over a medium-to-low heat for about 5 minutes then return the browned lamb pieces and any meat juices released to the pan. Stir well and gently simmer for 45 minutes–1 hour until the lamb is very tender.

Just before serving, stir in the double cream, lemon juice and rosewater. Heat gently and adjust the seasoning to taste. Serve immediately with warm Indian breads, such as naan or chapatti.

**SERVES 4**

1kg boneless leg of lamb
2 green chillies, deseeded and finely chopped
75g blanched almonds, lightly toasted
75g cashew nuts, lightly toasted
2 garlic cloves, peeled and finely chopped
2cm ginger, peeled and finely chopped
125ml water
3 tbsp vegetable oil
sea salt and freshly ground black pepper
1 cinnamon stick
4 cloves
1 bay leaf
2 tsp ground coriander
2 cardamom pods
2 onions, peeled and finely chopped
100ml natural yoghurt
pinch of saffron strands, soaked in 1 tbsp hot water
75ml double cream
1 tbsp lemon juice
1 tbsp rosewater

# Spiced pan-fried chicken with pumpkin purée

I made up this elegant dish as a way to thank food writer Seema Chandra after she kindly set me up on my first-ever journey across several north-western states in a quest to discover true Indian food. When I got back to New Delhi I wanted to cook her and her friends something special, but there was no point in cooking a truly authentic Indian meal since she can easily get that every day. This dish is the result of what I'd learnt from that epic trip, with one or two European cooking tricks thrown in for good measure. For example, I created a lovely aromatic sauce (not illustrated) made with chicken stock, an ingredient not generally used in Indian cooking. If you wish to cook this for a dinner party, prepare the different elements (i.e. make the pumpkin purée and sauce and marinate the chicken) so that you only need to cook the chicken and reheat everything just before serving. My Spiced aubergine and okra sauté (see page 146) is the perfect vegetable accompaniment for the chicken.

First, marinade the chicken. Put the chicken pieces into a large bowl and rub all over with a little salt and pepper. In another bowl, combine the papaya, cloves, cumin, turmeric, sugar, ginger, lime and orange juices and yoghurt, then add this to the chicken and toss well to coat. Cover the bowl with cling film and marinate in the fridge for at least a couple of hours.

## SERVES 4

1 whole chicken, jointed into 8 pieces
sea salt and freshly ground black pepper
2 tbsp finely grated raw green papaya
½ tsp ground cloves
1 tsp ground cumin
½ tsp ground turmeric
1 tsp caster sugar
1 tsp finely grated ginger
juice of 1 lime
juice of 1 orange
200ml natural yoghurt
2–3 tbsp corn flour
½–1 tsp hot chilli powder, to taste
vegetable oil, for frying
1 large hard-boiled egg, soaked in 2 tbsp water with a pinch of saffron added (optional)

**PUMPKIN PURÉE**
850g pumpkin or 1 large
  butternut squash
20g unsalted butter
2 star anise
1 cinnamon stick
2 bay leaves
1 tsp garam masala

Preheat the oven to 200°C/Fan 180°C/Gas 6. Peel the pumpkin, remove all the seeds and cut into small chunks. Melt the butter in a large roasting tin and add the star anise, cinnamon, bay leaves and garam masala. Fry for a minute until fragrant, then tip in the pumpkin chunks and season well. Toss well to coat the pumpkin in the spice butter, then place the roasting tin in the hot oven. Roast for 40–50 minutes until the pumpkin is very soft. Remove the whole spices and bay leaves and blend the pumpkin with a splash of water into a fine purée using a food processor. Taste and adjust the seasoning. Scrape the purée into a medium saucepan ready to reheat before serving.

For the aromatic sauce, heat the oil in a large saucepan and add the onion, garlic and some seasoning. Fry for 6–8 minutes, stirring occasionally, until the onion is soft and lightly golden brown. Tip in all the spices, dried chillies and bay leaves and fry for 1–2 minutes until they release a fragrant aroma. Add the tomatoes and coriander stalks and stir well. Cook for another 2–3 minutes before pouring in the stock. Bring to a gentle boil and cook for about 30–40 minutes until the sauce has reduced by two-thirds and is very flavourful. Strain the sauce through a fine sieve into a clean pan, pushing down on the solids to extract all the flavourful juices. Pour the cream into the pan and bring to a simmer. Taste and adjust the seasoning. If necessary, simmer the sauce until reduced to a light gravy consistency. Reheat before serving.

When you're ready to cook the chicken, preheat the oven to 200°C/Fan 180°C/Gas 6. Mix the corn flour with the chilli powder and some seasoning and toss with the marinated chicken to coat. Put a thin layer of oil in a wide, ovenproof frying pan and fry the chicken for 2 minutes on each side until golden brown. Transfer the pan to the hot oven and roast for about 14–16 minutes until firm and just cooked through.

To serve, place large spoonfuls of the pumpkin purée on warm serving plates and top with the pan-fried chicken. Spoon over some sauce and finely grate over the saffron-infused boiled egg, if using. If you wish, serve with some Spiced aubergine and okra sauté on the side.

**AROMATIC SAUCE**
1 tbsp vegetable oil
1 large onion, peeled and finely chopped
2 garlic cloves, peeled and finely chopped
5 cloves
1 cinnamon stick
1 tsp cumin seeds
3 cardamom pods, lightly crushed
½ tsp fenugreek
1 tsp hot chilli powder, or to taste
1 tsp ground turmeric
2 whole dried red chillies
2 bay leaves
4 ripe plum tomatoes, chopped
handful of coriander stalks
1 litre good-quality chicken stock
150ml double cream

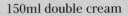

# Punjabi masala chops

Punjabi cooking is perhaps the Indian cuisine with which we are most familiar, as the vast majority of Indian restaurants in Britain offer food from this region. This style of cooking favours dishes that use tomatoes, and in this recipe they form an integral part of the sauce. Although not traditional, I prefer to seal off the chops before adding them to the sauce so they caramelise and add a meaty, savoury flavour.

Trim off any excess fat around the chops, leaving on a thin, even layer, and season well. Put the ginger, garlic, chilli and a tablespoon or two of water into a food processor or blender and blitz to wet paste. Heat 2 tablespoons of oil in a wide, heavy-based pan, and when you can feel a strong heat rising, add the lamb chops and fry for about 1–2 minutes on each side, until lightly browned all over. Remove the chops from the pan and set aside.

Add the remaining oil to the pan and add the onions, garam masala, cumin, cayenne pepper and chilli powder. Stir well and sauté gently for 3–4 minutes or until the onions have softened slightly and the spices are fragrant. Add the ginger and garlic paste and cook for another couple of minutes. Increase the heat and add the browned chops, tomatoes, lemon juice and salt. Bring to the boil, then reduce the heat to a simmer and partially cover the pan. Simmer, stirring occasionally, for 50 minutes–1 hour or until the meat is tender and the sauce thick. Over a low heat, gradually stir in the yoghurt and simmer for a few minutes. Taste and adjust the seasoning.

Arrange the chops on a warm platter and garnish with coriander leaves. Serve immediately with warm breads or plain basmati rice.

**SERVES 4**

8 lamb chops
3cm ginger, peeled and
  roughly chopped
4 garlic cloves, peeled
  and roughly chopped
1 red chilli, deseeded
  and roughly chopped
3 tbsp vegetable oil
2 onions, peeled and
  finely chopped
2 tsp garam masala
1 tsp ground cumin
1½ tsp cayenne pepper
1 tsp mild chilli powder
800g chopped plum
  tomatoes
2 tbsp lemon juice
1 tsp sea salt, or to taste
450ml natural yoghurt
coriander leaves, to
  garnish

# Butter chicken

**SERVES 4**

800g boneless and skinless chicken thighs, cut into 3–4cm pieces

2 garlic cloves, peeled and finely crushed

2cm ginger, peeled and finely grated

½ tsp fine sea salt

½ tsp hot chilli powder

1½ tbsp lemon juice

75ml natural yoghurt

½ tsp garam masala

½ tsp ground turmeric

1 tsp ground cumin

1–2 tbsp vegetable oil, for brushing

**SAUCE**

1½ tbsp ghee or melted unsalted butter

2 garlic cloves, peeled and finely chopped

2cm ginger, peeled and finely chopped

1 cardamom pod, seeds lightly crushed

2 cloves

1 tsp ground coriander

1 tsp garam masala

1 tsp ground turmeric

1 tsp hot chilli powder, or to taste

275ml tomato purée

1 tbsp lemon juice

40g unsalted butter

100ml double cream

1 tbsp chopped coriander, to garnish

Butter chicken, or *murgh makhani*, was one of the first dishes I tasted when I went to India. Its origins can be traced back to Moghul times, but the dish and its history is most closely associated with Delhi's famous Moti Mahal restaurant, where I had the pleasure of eating this fantastic dish. Over time, numerous chefs have attempted to emulate the rich buttery sauce, and flavours vary slightly between restaurants. This is my version of the classic dish.

Place the chicken in a bowl with the garlic, ginger, salt, chilli powder and lemon juice. Mix, cover with cling film and chill for 30 minutes. Mix together the yoghurt, garam masala, turmeric and cumin and add to the chicken, making sure that each piece is well coated with the mixture. Cover again and chill for 3–4 hours.

Preheat the oven to 180°C/Fan 160°C/Gas 4. Put the marinated chicken pieces on a grill rack set on a baking tray and bake for 8–10 minutes. Brush the chicken pieces with a little oil and turn them over. Bake for another 10–12 minutes until just cooked through.

For the sauce, heat the ghee or butter in a pan and add the garlic and ginger. Fry for a minute or so then add the cardamom, cloves, coriander, garam masala, turmeric and chilli powder. Stir well and fry for 1–2 minutes until they give off a lovely aroma. Stir in the tomato purée and lemon juice and cook for another couple of minutes. Add the chicken pieces to the sauce and stir well to coat. Finally, add the butter and cream and stir continuously until the butter has melted and the sauce is smooth. Taste and adjust the seasoning. Transfer to a warm bowl and serve hot, garnished with chopped coriander.

# Guinea fowl in tomato and coconut curry

Not surprisingly, this curry comes from South India, where the use of coconut and tomatoes is common-place. The Indians would use chicken, but guinea fowl breasts make a lovely alternative. Although it doesn't take long to prepare, this dish is best prepared ahead so that the guinea fowl has time to absorb the flavours of the curry. Reheat gently and serve with Coconut rice or a Plain dosa (see pages 169 and 194).

Cut the guinea fowl breasts into bite-sized pieces and rub all over with a pinch each of salt and pepper. Heat 2 tablespoons of oil in a large frying pan over a medium heat. In batches, fry the guinea fowl breasts lightly for 1–2 minutes on each side until lightly browned all over. Remove the meat from the pan to a plate as you brown each batch. Set aside.

Add the remaining oil to the same pan followed by the cinnamon, cloves and curry leaves. Cook for a minute or until the spices become very fragrant. Stir in the garam masala and chilli powder, and after 30 seconds add the onion and garlic. Sauté gently for 6–8 minutes until the onion is softened but not browned. Add the tomatoes and grated coconut, if using, then season lightly with salt and continue to cook for another 3–4 minutes.

Pour in the coconut milk and bring to the boil briefly. Reduce the heat and return the guinea fowl to the pan. Simmer for 5–10 minutes until the meat is just cooked through. Serve immediately.

**SERVES 4**

4 skinless guinea fowl breasts
sea salt and freshly ground black pepper
3 tbsp vegetable oil
½ cinnamon stick
¼ tsp ground cloves
4 curry leaves
1 tsp garam masala
1 tsp hot chilli powder
1 onion, peeled and finely chopped
2 garlic cloves, peeled and finely chopped
500g tomatoes, skinned and finely chopped
100g freshly grated coconut (optional)
400ml tin coconut milk

# Chicken badami

**SERVES 4**

500g boneless and skinless chicken (thighs or breasts), cut into 2cm pieces

4 garlic cloves, peeled and finely chopped

2cm ginger, peeled and finely grated

1 tbsp lemon juice

sea salt and freshly ground black pepper

25g slivered almonds

2 tbsp ghee or melted unsalted butter

2 onions, peeled and finely chopped

1 cinnamon stick

4 cardamom pods, lightly crushed

3 cloves

1 tsp ground cumin

1 tsp ground coriander

1 tsp ground turmeric

50g finely ground almonds

300ml natural yoghurt

*Badami* means almond, and this dish is typical of Moghlai cuisine, which favours using raw nuts to make a thick and creamy gravy. Serve this dish with plenty of naan bread, as you want to mop up every last bit of the flavourful almond sauce.

Put the chicken pieces into a large bowl with the garlic, ginger, lemon juice and some seasoning. Mix well, cover the bowl with cling film and leave to marinate in the fridge for a few hours or overnight.

Place a large frying pan over a medium heat, add the slivered almonds and dry-toast them until they are a light golden brown, remembering to toss them every once in a while to avoid burning the nuts. Tip on to a plate and leave to cool.

Return the pan to the heat and add the ghee or butter and the onions. Cook over a medium heat, stirring occasionally, for 6–8 minutes or until golden brown. Add the cinnamon, cardamom and cloves and fry for 2–3 minutes before adding the cumin, coriander, turmeric and ground almonds. Add the chicken to the pan and stir well to coat the meat in the spices. Turn the heat up slightly and stir frequently until the chicken turns opaque.

Reduce the heat to low and gradually stir in the yoghurt. Bring to a slow simmer, cover the pan and cook for another 20–30 minutes, stirring once or twice, until the chicken is tender.

When ready to serve, ladle the chicken into a serving bowl and sprinkle over the toasted almonds to garnish.

# Malabar duck

Malabar is an area of Kerala famed for its use of spices, and the region produces rich and delicious food. Pure coconut oil is used a lot in southern Indian cooking, so if you can get hold of some it will add to the authenticity of the curry. Whilst almonds are widely used in northern Indian cooking, cashew nuts are favoured in the south, and in this dish they add a distinctive flavour to the sweet and sour sauce.

Trim the duck breasts to neaten the edges and rub them all over with the ginger, garlic, turmeric and some salt and pepper. Cover the dish with cling film and chill for at least 4 hours.

Heat half the oil in a heavy-based pan until hot. Fry the shallots with some seasoning for 4–6 minutes until soft and lightly golden. Add the chilli powder, coriander and garam masala and cook for another 30 seconds until fragrant. Tip in the cashew nuts and raisins or sultanas and cook for a few more minutes. Pour in the coconut milk and bring to a gentle simmer.

In a wide frying pan, heat the remaining oil with the curry leaves then fry the duck breasts for 1–2 minutes on each side until browned. Transfer the duck breasts to the sauce to finish cooking and add the cherry tomatoes. Simmer for another 3–5 minutes until the duck breasts are cooked through. Serve immediately with rice.

**SERVES 4**

4 skinless duck breasts, about 200g each
3cm ginger, peeled and finely grated
3 garlic cloves, peeled and finely crushed
½ tsp ground turmeric
sea salt and freshly ground black pepper
3 tbsp coconut or vegetable oil
5 shallots, peeled and finely chopped
1 tsp hot chilli powder
1 tsp ground coriander
1 tsp garam masala
25g cashew nuts, finely chopped
1 tbsp raisins or sultanas
200ml coconut milk
6–8 curry leaves
100g cherry tomatoes, halved

# Spiced leg of lamb wrapped with spring onions

**SERVES 6**

large bunch long spring
  onions, about 10–12
4 large or 6 small ready-
  made chapattis
2.75kg leg of lamb,
  boned, butterflied
  and rolled
2 large banana leaves

**MARINADE**

4 garlic cloves, peeled
  and roughly chopped
2 tbsp ghee or melted
  unsalted butter
1 tsp sea salt, or to taste
1 tsp hot chilli powder
1 tsp ground coriander
1 tsp garam masala
1 large onion, peeled
  and roughly chopped
3 ripe plum tomatoes,
  roughly chopped
small bunch coriander,
  leaves and stems
  roughly chopped
juice of ½ lemon
  (or 2 tbsp ground
  kachri)

**DRY SPICE RUB**

1 tsp fine sea salt
1 tsp hot chilli powder
2 tsp garam masala

This is my modern take on a Rajasthani classic called *khud khargosh*, an ingenious recipe for pit-roasting meat in the desert using only natural resources: hot coals and desert sand. I was shown how to make the original recipe by the nephew of the Maharajah of Jodhpur and was told that the dish was traditionally made with hare (*khargosh*) until the hunting ban in the 1970s, which led to the popular use of goat or mutton. The original tenderiser for the meat came in the form of *kachri*, which resembles a small, yellowish-brown melon growing wild in the desert areas. Cooked fresh, kachri tastes of a mildly sour melon but it is also frequently dried and ground into a powder. It is rarely found outside of Rajasthan in either form, but I find that a little lemon juice provides a similar effect.

First, make the marinade. Put all the ingredients into a food processor and blend to a wet paste, stopping the machine to scrape down the bowl of the processor a few times. Transfer the paste to a bowl and set aside. In another small bowl, mix together the ingredients for the dry spice rub.

Lightly blanch the spring onions in a pan of boiling water for about a minute to soften them. Refresh under cold running water and drain well.

Preheat the oven to 200°C/Fan 180°C /Gas 6. Lay out four long strings along a work surface, about 5cm apart. Overlap the chapattis on top to form a rough rectangle that is wide and long enough to wrap around the leg of lamb. Arrange the blanched spring onions in a single layer on top.

Open out the lamb, skinned-side up, on a chopping board and sprinkle all over with the dry spice rub. Turn the lamb around and lay on top of the spring onions. Spread the marinade all along the boned side of the meat. Roll the lamb into a log then wrap the chapattis and spring onions around the joint and secure with the strings. Put the whole thing on two large, overlapping banana leaves that have been softened slightly over a low flame (see page 70). Wrap the leaves around the lamb like a parcel, again securing with string.

Put on a large roasting tin and roast for about 1¼–1¾ hours until the lamb has just cooked through. To check, insert a metal skewer into the centre of the joint for 10 seconds then remove and feel it against your wrist. It should feel hot. Remove the lamb from the oven and leave to rest for about 15–20 minutes.

To serve, unwrap the banana leaves and remove the strings. Unwrap the chapattis and transfer the lamb to a carving board. Slice thickly then serve each slice on a chapatti, which would have absorbed some marinade and the flavourful juices from the meat during cooking. To add some fresh flavours, serve with a sliced tomato, cucumber, onion and mint salad.

# Tribal chicken casserole with tamarind

This is my take on a rustic dish that was cooked for me during my stay with the amazing Bastar tribe in the state of Chhattisgarh. There, meals are made using only fresh ingredients sourced from the land. As this dish exemplifies, no edible part from an animal is wasted: the whole chicken, including the heart and liver, is cooked in a hearty stew that vaguely resembles a layered Lancashire hotpot.

Tip the garlic, ginger, chillies, tamarind paste, lime juice, turmeric and some salt and pepper in a food processor and blend to a fine wet paste. Scrape the paste into a bowl and stir in the chopped tomatoes and oil. In a separate bowl, combine the onions and potatoes and season well.

Preheat the oven to 180°C/Fan 160°C/Gas 4. Cover the base of a lightly oiled ovenproof casserole (with a lid) with a third of the potato and onion mixture and sprinkle over some seasoning. Spread a layer of the ginger and garlic paste on top. Layer over half the chicken pieces and scatter over the chopped heart and livers, if using. Season lightly then spread a layer of the ginger and garlic paste over the meat. Continue to add the layers until the ingredients are used up, finishing with a final layer of ginger and garlic paste. Scatter over the tamarind pods, if using, then sprinkle the water on top.

Cover the casserole and bake for 50 minutes–1 hour until the chicken is cooked. Bring the casserole straight to the table to serve. Remove the tamarind pods before serving, if you added them.

**SERVES 4**

4 garlic cloves, peeled and roughly chopped
3cm ginger, peeled and roughly chopped
2 red chillies, deseeded and roughly chopped
2 tbsp tamarind paste
juice of 1 lime
1 tsp ground turmeric
sea salt and freshly ground black pepper
4 tomatoes, skinned and chopped
2 tbsp vegetable oil
2 onions, peeled and thinly sliced
400g baby or new potatoes, thinly sliced
1 medium chicken, jointed into 8 pieces, with heart and livers, chopped (optional)
2–3 whole tamarind pods (optional)
4 tbsp water

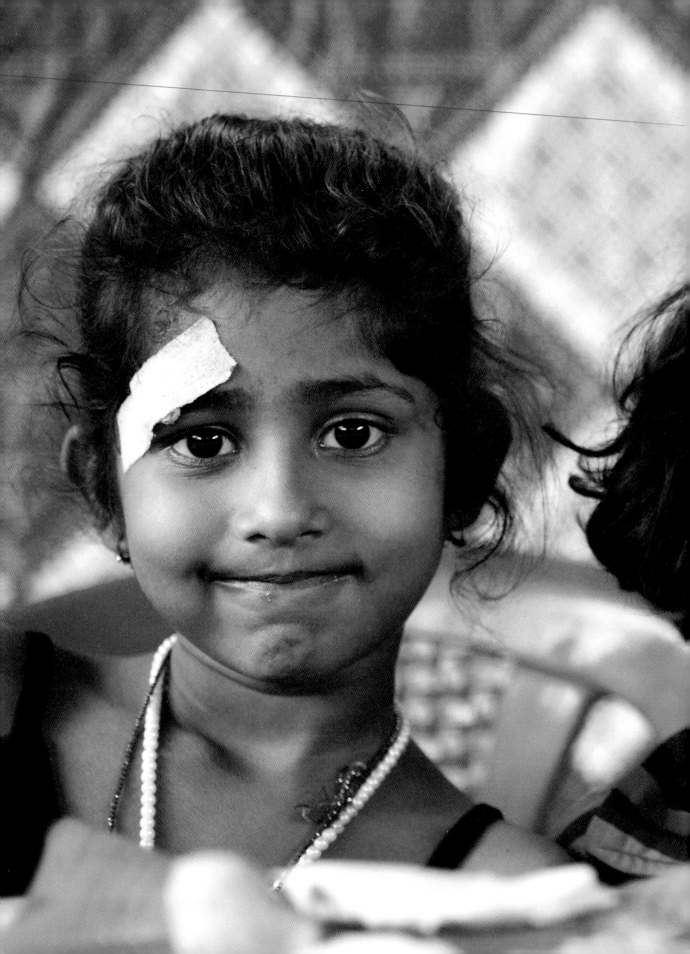

# Quail tandoori

**SERVES 4**
4–8 oven-ready quails
1 tsp sea salt
juice of 1 lemon

**MARINADE**
3–4cm ginger, peeled
  and chopped
4 garlic cloves, peeled
  and chopped
1 large onion, peeled
  and finely chopped
400ml natural yoghurt
1½ tbsp tomato purée
½ tsp garam masala
1 tsp hot chilli powder,
  or to taste
1 tsp ground paprika
1 tsp ground cumin
1 tsp ground coriander
a couple of drops each
  of natural red and
  yellow food colouring
  (optional)

Tandoori chicken is probably one of the most recognised of all Indian dishes. The heat inside a proper tandoor is so intense that a whole marinated chicken can be baked in minutes to a succulent and moist finish, even though very little oil or fat is used. When using a domestic oven, you're more likely to get this result with small marinated quails. The secret is to marinate the birds for at least 4 hours or ideally overnight. I'm not a fan of using food colouring, but if you wish to add some to the marinade, please get a natural one. If you're serving this as part of a multi-course meal, one quail per person should suffice; otherwise serve two quails each.

Rub the quails with salt and place them in a large dish. Squeeze over the lemon juice, cover with cling film and chill for about 30 minutes.

Meanwhile, make the tandoori marinade. Put the ginger, garlic and onion in a food processor with a tablespoon of water and blitz to a fine wet paste. Tip into a large bowl and add the yoghurt, tomato purée, garam masala, chilli powder, paprika, cumin, coriander and food colouring, if using. Mix well. Coat the quails with the marinade and chill for 4 hours or overnight.

Preheat the oven to the highest setting. Remove the quails from the fridge and place on a baking tray, breast-side up. Coat with any remaining marinade and cook for 18–20 minutes or until just cooked through. The juices should run clear when you pierce the thickest part of each quail with a skewer. Serve with warm chapatti or naan breads and some sliced onions, tomatoes and lemon wedges.

# Chicken and papaya curry

**SERVES 4**

500–600g boneless
  and skinless
  chicken thighs
1 tsp ground turmeric
sea salt and freshly
  ground black pepper
2 tbsp mustard or
  vegetable oil
2 medium onions,
  peeled and finely
  chopped
3cm ginger, peeled and
  finely grated
3 garlic cloves, peeled
  and finely chopped
1 green chilli, deseeded
  and finely chopped
  (optional)
150ml water
6 tbsp finely chopped
  raw green papaya
juice of 1 lime
small handful of
  coriander leaves,
  to garnish

This isn't so much a curry in the traditional sense of the word, but more like a light and flavourful casserole with chicken and papaya as the star ingredients. I cooked it as part of a recipe challenge upon returning from the northeast of India. The food there is lighter and the ingredients used are mostly fresh. The papaya acts not only as a tenderiser but also as a sauce thickener. If you prefer a smooth sauce, purée the papaya in a food processor instead of chopping it. I didn't add chilli in the original recipe, but I have included one as an option here, should you want a little heat in the curry.

Cut the chicken thighs into bite-sized pieces and mix them with the turmeric and some seasoning. Set aside.

Heat the oil in a wide heavy-based pan until hot. Add the onions, ginger, garlic and chilli, if using. Fry for 4–5 minutes, stirring frequently, until the onions begin to soften. Add the chicken pieces and mix well. Fry over a high heat for a few minutes then add the water and papaya and bring to a simmer. Cook gently for 15–20 minutes until the chicken is tender and the sauce is thick.

Finally, add the lime juice and seasoning to taste. Transfer to a warm serving bowl, garnish with the coriander leaves and serve while still hot.

# Venison stew

I cooked this after an exhausting day hunting with the Konyaks, a tribe of hunters in Nagaland, at the northeastern tip of India. There was a ritual to the hunt and the butchering process. Tradition dictates that the deer's head and right thigh is given to the successful hunter and the left thigh is given to the chief. As an honoured guest, I was presented with the saddle (which, surprisingly, is not favoured over any other cut). The remaining parts were divided among the other hunters. I cooked the saddle at the communal kitchen, where I had at my disposal some fresh local vegetables, a little honey and a bottle of beer. (Dried spices are not common in this part of the world.) The resulting stew was a departure from the richly spiced curries that I'd been eating during the trip, but it was delicious and comforting.

Cut the venison into 2.5–3-cm pieces, then season all over with salt and pepper. Heat half the oil in a wide pan until hot. Fry the venison pieces in several batches for about 2 minutes on each side until browned all over. Transfer each batch to a plate and set aside. Put the remaining oil in the pan and fry the onions, carrots, chillies and garlic over a medium-to-high heat. Fry, stirring frequently, for 5–6 minutes until the vegetables soften. Add the flour and stir for about 2 minutes.

Pour in the beer and add the tomatoes, coriander stems and honey. Return the venison to the pan and simmer very gently for about 20 minutes until the venison is just cooked through and tender. Taste and adjust the seasoning. Just before serving, stir in the coriander leaves. Enjoy the stew with plenty of plain steamed rice.

**SERVES 4**

1kg boneless saddle of venison
sea salt and freshly ground black pepper
4 tbsp mustard or vegetable oil
2 onions, peeled and chopped
2 medium carrots, peeled and chopped
3 red chillies, deseeded and chopped
3 garlic cloves, peeled and finely chopped
2 tbsp plain flour
330ml bottle light beer
3–4 plum tomatoes, peeled and chopped
small bunch coriander, stems and leaves chopped separately
1½ tbsp honey, or to taste

# Vegetarian

Rajasthani red lentil curry

Maharashtrian spiced cabbage

Mixed vegetable undhiyo

Andhra banana curry

Egg curry

Black-eyed bean curry

Spiced aubergine and okra sauté

Curried okra

Saag aloo

Cauliflower tandoori

Sweet potatoes with panch phoran

Stir-fried butternut squash with dried chilli

Spicy cucumber and coconut salad

# Rajasthani red lentil curry

SERVES 4

225g split pigeon pea
  lentils (tuvar dal) or
  red split lentils,
  washed
2 cloves
½ cinnamon stick
4 black peppercorns
1 litre water
2.5cm ginger, peeled
  and chopped
3 garlic cloves, peeled
  and chopped
3 tbsp ghee or melted
  unsalted butter
2 onions, peeled and
  finely chopped
3 tomatoes, skinned
  and finely chopped
2 tsp garam masala
2 tsp hot chilli powder,
  to taste
1 tsp ground turmeric
½ tsp sea salt, or to taste
2 tbsp double cream
3 green chillies, slit in
  half lengthways

This dish is based on the lentil curry *dal baati*, a popular Rajasthani dish that in India is almost always served with baked round buns made from wheat and gram flours and ghee. I've chosen to leave out the *baati* buns to keep the recipe simple, and also because I think the curry is equally delicious eaten with plain naan or chapatti generously brushed with melted butter. You can make the curry with only one type of lentil (as I have) or use a mixture of tuvar (dark ochre-coloured split and skinned pigeon peas) and urad dals, although you may need to adjust the cooking times slightly, adding 15–20 minutes more.

Place the lentils in a saucepan with the cloves, cinnamon, peppercorns and water. Bring to the boil and skim off any scum and froth that rises to the surface of the liquid. Reduce the heat, partially cover the pan and simmer for 25–30 minutes until the lentils are soft and have broken down.

Put the ginger and garlic into a small food processor. Add a tablespoon of water and blitz to a paste. Heat the ghee or butter in a pan, add the onions and fry for 6–8 minutes, stirring occasionally, until lightly browned. Add the garlic and ginger paste, tomatoes, garam masala, chilli powder and turmeric to the pan.

After 2–3 minutes, tip the cooked lentils into the pan, season well with salt and leave to simmer for 8–10 minutes until thick. Stir through the cream and green chillies; then you are ready to serve.

# Maharashtrian spiced cabbage

This is a typical quick and easy vegetable stir-fry from Maharashtra, which goes well with pretty much any fish or meat dish. I particularly enjoy it with a biryani. It is also lovely as a side dish for roast meat – just think of our roast venison with spiced braised cabbage. For a variation, add a few nuggets of jaggery or light brown soft sugar and some fresh lemon juice to give the cabbage some sweetness and acidity.

Finely shred the cabbage and set aside.

Heat the oil in a wide pan over a medium heat. Add the mustard seeds and when they begin to pop, tip in the curry leaves and urad dal. When the urad dal begins to turn a light golden brown, after about 2–3 minutes, add the sliced onion and sauté gently for 6–8 minutes, or until soft.

Add the cabbage, turmeric, cumin, water and a generous pinch of salt to the pan. If you're using the grated coconut, add this now. Stir well and simmer for 5–7 minutes until the cabbage is cooked but still retains some bite. Taste and adjust the seasoning, then serve in a warm bowl.

**SERVES 4**
500g green or
  white cabbage
2 tbsp vegetable oil
1½ tsp black mustard
  seeds
8–10 curry leaves
1½ tsp urad dal
1 large onion, peeled
  and finely sliced
½ tsp ground turmeric
1 tsp ground cumin
50ml water
sea salt, to taste
3 tbsp freshly grated
  coconut (optional)

# Mixed vegetable undhiyo

**SERVES 4**

6–8 baby potatoes, peeled or just scrubbed, if you prefer

4–5 small Indian aubergines (or 1 medium), trimmed

1 small sweet potato (or yam), peeled

1 large carrot, peeled

1 large unripe banana, peeled

50g green beans, topped and tailed

2 tbsp vegetable oil

1 tsp mustard seeds

½ tsp carom seeds

¼ tsp asafoetida (optional)

½ tsp sea salt, or to taste

½ tsp ground turmeric

½ tsp ground cumin

½ tsp ground coriander

200ml water

small handful of toasted coconut shavings, to garnish (optional)

**MASALA PASTE**

4 garlic cloves, peeled and chopped

2.5cm ginger, peeled and chopped

3 green chillies, deseeded and chopped

75g grated coconut, thawed, if frozen

1 tbsp chopped coriander leaves

This tasty mixed-vegetable casserole originates from Gujarat in western India. It is mainly cooked in winter, but the ingredients may vary depending on what is available locally. I've sampled a couple of versions of the dish during my trip to India: one was wet with a thick greenish gravy; the other was a dry casserole of colourful vegetables, dry spices and grated coconut. This recipe is similar to the latter version, which I much preferred. Use any combination of vegetables you like, but do include several root vegetables to give the dish a hearty, starchy base.

First, make the masala paste. Put all the paste ingredients into a food processor. Add 3 tablespoons of water and blitz to form a thick paste.

Cut the potatoes, aubergines, sweet potato or yam, carrot and banana into bite-sized pieces, and the beans into 2cm pieces. Keep each ingredient separate.

Heat the oil in a large pan. Add the mustard seeds, carom seeds and asafoetida, if using. When the seeds begin to pop, add the masala paste. Cook for 2–3 minutes, stirring frequently. Put the potatoes and carrots into the pan and cook for 5 minutes before adding the rest of the vegetables, salt and the remaining ground spices. Fry over a high heat for 5 minutes, then reduce the heat, add the water and stir. Cover and simmer for about 10–15 minutes or until the vegetables are cooked through and tender. Transfer to a warm serving bowl and garnish with a sprinkling of coconut shavings, if you wish.

# Andhra banana curry

Raw bananas regularly feature in Indian vegetarian dishes, and this exceptional curry is a must-try. It has well-balanced flavours with a warming heat from the spices, some sweetness from the bananas and a little acidity from the tamarind paste.

Put the garlic, ginger, urad dal and a splash of water in a blender or food processor and blitz to a fine wet paste. Scrape into a small bowl and set aside.

Heat the oil in a karahi or wok. Add the curry leaves and mustard seeds and cook for a minute until the seeds begin to splutter. Add the paste that you made earlier to the pan, along with the chilli powder and turmeric.

Fry the mixture for 4–6 minutes before adding the tamarind paste to the pan. Pour in the water and stir well. Bring to the boil, then reduce the heat and simmer for 2–3 minutes. Add the bananas to the pan and cook, stirring occasionally, for 6–8 minutes or until the sauce has thickened.

Transfer the banana curry to a warm bowl, stir in the coconut and serve immediately.

**SERVES 4**

4 garlic cloves, peeled and roughly chopped
3cm ginger, peeled and roughly chopped
1 tsp urad dal
2 tbsp vegetable oil
8 curry leaves
1 tsp black mustard seeds
1 tsp hot chilli powder
½ tsp ground turmeric
1½ tbsp tamarind paste
400ml water
6 large unripe bananas, peeled and cut into 4cm pieces
2 tbsp freshly grated coconut

# Egg curry

**SERVES 4**

6 large eggs
1 tsp ground cumin
1 tsp ground coriander
1 tsp ground turmeric
1 tsp red chilli powder
½ tsp garam masala
1–2 tbsp water
2 tbsp vegetable oil
1 onion, peeled and
  finely chopped
400g tomatoes, skinned
  and chopped
1 tsp fine sea salt
handful of coriander
  leaves, roughly
  chopped

An egg curry is the ideal food for frugal times: it is tasty, economical and nutritious but, more importantly, it is a crucial source of protein for vegetarians. As this curry exemplifies, the Indians have a special flair for transforming something as basic as a boiled egg into a delicious dish. Serve with any type of Indian bread or plain rice, but I find Jeera or Tamarind rice make good accompaniments (see pages 186 and 166).

Put the eggs in a medium saucepan and cover them with cold water. When the water begins to simmer, set the timer to 10 minutes for hard-boiled eggs. Remove the eggs with a slotted spoon and cool them in a bowl of iced water. Drain, then gently peel away the shells. Slice them in half and set aside.

In a small bowl, mix together the ground cumin, coriander, turmeric, chilli powder and garam masala. Add enough water to create a wet paste with a slow-dropping consistency.

Heat the oil in a wide pan. Add the onion and fry for 6–8 minutes, stirring occasionally, until golden brown. Tip the spice paste into the pan and cook for 2–3 minutes before adding the chopped tomatoes and salt. Stir in the coriander and simmer for 4–5 minutes. If the sauce seems too dry, add a splash of water.

Carefully lower the boiled eggs into the pan and simmer gently until heated through, trying not to stir too much so that the egg yolks remain with the whites. When hot, transfer into a warm bowl and serve immediately.

# Black-eyed bean curry

This is one of my favourite bean curries – it is very flavourful and you can eat it plainly with some rice or flat breads and a raita for a simple meal. From my travels I have acquired a neat Indian trick to make dried pulses easier to digest: leave them to soak well overnight and then cook them with a combination of ginger, turmeric (preferably fresh) and a little pinch of asafoetida.

Drain the soaked black-eyed beans and place them in a saucepan with the water. Bring to the boil and skim off the froth that rises to the surface. Reduce the heat to a simmer, partially cover and cook, stirring occasionally, until the beans are tender but not mushy. It should take about 30 minutes or so. Drain and set aside.

While the beans are cooking, heat the oil in a heavy-based pan and tip in the cumin seeds and cinnamon stick. When the spices are fragrant, add the onions and garlic. Fry for 6–8 minutes, stirring frequently, until the onions are soft and a dark golden brown. If they begin to burn, add a splash of water to the pan.

Add the ground cumin, coriander, cayenne pepper and a generous pinch of salt to the pan. Stir for a minute then tip in the chopped tomatoes and asafoetida, if using. Stir well, cover, and turn the heat down to a simmer. After about 10 minutes, add the cooked black-eyed beans and leave to simmer, uncovered, for a further 20 minutes. Taste and adjust the seasoning. Stir in the chopped coriander just before serving.

**SERVES 4**

250g dried black-eyed
   beans (*lobia*), soaked
   in plenty of water
   overnight
1.5 litres water
3 tbsp vegetable oil
1½ tsp cumin seeds
1 cinnamon stick
2 medium onions,
   peeled and chopped
4 garlic cloves, peeled
   and finely chopped
1½ tsp ground cumin
1 tsp ground coriander
1 tsp cayenne pepper
sea salt
350g tomatoes, skinned
   and chopped
pinch of asafoetida
   (optional)
2 tbsp chopped
   coriander

# Spiced aubergine and okra sauté

**SERVES 4**

1 medium aubergine
sea salt and freshly
  ground black pepper
1 tsp caster sugar
vegetable oil, for frying
1 large onion, peeled
  and chopped
1 tsp ground cumin
½ tsp ground turmeric
300g okra, roughly
  sliced
1 red chilli, deseeded
  and finely sliced
handful of mint leaves
handful of coriander
  leaves

Before I went to India I had a great dislike for okra, or 'lady's fingers' – even going as far as banning it from my restaurants. I found its slimy texture unappealing and didn't think much of what it added to a cooked dish. After my trip I still can't say I've been converted to eating it regularly, but I am more open to cooking it in different ways. I created this dish to accompany to my Spiced pan-fried chicken with pumpkin purée (see page 109), and it has been very well-received, judging from the empty plates that came back.

Chop the aubergine into 1cm dice and place them in a colander. Toss with a generous pinch each of salt and pepper and the sugar. Leave them in the colander in the sink for about 20 minutes, by which time the salt will have drawn out some moisture from the aubergines.

Heat about 3cm of oil in a heavy-based pan until hot. Fry the aubergines for 2–3 minutes until soft. Remove with a slotted spoon and place in a sieve set over a bowl. Press down lightly with the slotted spoon to squeeze out the excess oil from the aubergines.

Pour out most of the oil from the pan, leaving about a tablespoon or so. Add the onion and some seasoning and fry for 5–6 minutes until translucent and soft. Add the cumin and turmeric and fry for a minute to toast the spices. Tip in the okra, chilli and aubergine and stir well. Cook for 2–3 minutes until the okra is just tender and the aubergines are hot. Season well to taste. Stir through the mint and coriander leaves, take the pan off the heat and serve immediately.

# Curried okra

This is a dry okra dish and the trick is to stir-fry the vegetable quickly so that it gets cooked without too much moisture, which helps to prevent it becoming too slimy. A little acidity, in the form of lemon juice or tart tomatoes, also helps to reduce the sliminess of the finished dish. Young tender pods are best, as they do not require much cooking.

Place the garlic and chillies into a food processor or blender with 2–3 tablespoons of water. Blend to form a smooth paste. Scrape the mixture into a small bowl and add the cumin, turmeric and coriander. Wash the okra under running water and pat dry with kitchen paper. Trim away the stems just above the ridge and cut into 2cm pieces.

Heat the oil in a frying pan and add the paste that you have just made. Allow the spices to cook out for 4–5 minutes before adding the okra, salt, sugar and lemon juice. Stir well to coat the okra in the spices and stir-fry gently for 6–8 minutes, or until the okra is tender and the mixture is quite dry. Remove from the heat and serve immediately as part of a main meal.

**SERVES 4–6**

4 garlic cloves, peeled
  and roughly chopped
2 green chillies,
  deseeded and roughly
  chopped
2 tsp ground cumin
1 tsp ground turmeric
1 tsp ground coriander
400g okra
3 tbsp vegetable oil
1 tsp salt, or to taste
1 tsp sugar
juice of ½ lemon

# Saag aloo

This spinach (*saag*) and potato (*aloo*) dish is perhaps one of the most popular Indian side dishes in the UK. I certainly always ordered a portion with my Friday-night curries. It is ideal eaten with rice, a lentil dal and another vegetable, meat or fish main course.

**SERVES 4**

400g fresh spinach
  leaves
2 tbsp vegetable oil
pinch of asafoetida
  (optional)
1 tsp black mustard
  seeds
1 tsp onion seeds
1 onion, peeled and
  finely sliced
3 garlic cloves, peeled
  and finely chopped
1 green chilli, deseeded
  and finely sliced
600g floury potatoes,
  peeled and diced into
  2.5cm cubes
1 tsp sea salt, or to taste
½ tsp cayenne pepper
squeeze of lemon juice,
  to taste

Bring a pan of salted water to the boil. Add the spinach and blanch for a minute. Drain in a colander and refresh under cold running water. With the spinach still in the colander, use a large spoon to squeeze out the excess liquid. Lay the leaves out on a chopping board and chop coarsely. Set aside.

Heat the oil in a large frying pan. Add the asafoetida, if using, and the mustard and onion seeds. When the seeds begin to pop, add the onion, garlic and chilli. After 3–4 minutes, tip the diced potatoes into the pan and season with salt and cayenne pepper. Fry for a couple of minutes over a high heat, stirring frequently.

Add 4–5 tablespoons of water, cover and gently cook over a low heat for 20–30 minutes until the potatoes are tender, stirring or shaking the pan every so often so that the potatoes don't stick to the base and burn. If the mixture looks too dry, add a little more water.

Uncover the pan and add the blanched spinach along with the lemon juice. Give the mixture a stir then cook for 1–2 minutes until the spinach is heated through. Transfer to a warm plate and serve.

# Cauliflower tandoori

Many Indian villages have community ovens where families can take their marinated meats, fish and vegetables to cook in blazing hot tandoors. This dish would literally take minutes to bake in a traditional tandoor, without the need to blanch the cauliflower beforehand (this prevents the vegetable drying out). This recipe achieves a similar result using a domestic oven, but you can also try grilling the cauliflower on a hot barbecue to add a slightly smoky element to the dish.

Blanch the cauliflowers in a pot of salted water for 2–3 minutes until barely tender. Drain and refresh in a bowl of iced water. Drain again.

In a large mixing bowl, combine all the remaining ingredients to make a marinade. Add the blanched cauliflower florets and toss well to coat. Place them on a lightly oiled baking tray and loosely cover with foil or cling film. Chill for a few hours to allow the flavours to infuse.

When ready to cook, preheat the oven to 200°C/Fan 180°C/Gas 6. Uncover the baking tray and place in the oven for 8–10 minutes until the cauliflower is golden brown and tender when pierced with a knife.

While the cauliflower is in the oven, fry the onion rings. Heat the oil in a pan until hot then add the onion rings, tomato purée and a pinch each of salt and pepper. When the onions are soft and golden brown, after about 6–8 minutes, and with the occasional stir, add the garam and chaat masalas. Stir well and fry for another minute. Take the pan off the heat and keep warm. Serve the cauliflower tandoori with the onions spread over the top and garnished with the coriander leaves.

**SERVES 4**

4 baby cauliflowers, trimmed and cut into large florets
300ml thick Greek-style yoghurt
3cm ginger, peeled and finely grated
3 garlic cloves, peeled and finely crushed
½ tsp sea salt, or to taste
½ tsp ground turmeric
1 tsp hot chilli powder, or to taste
1½ tsp garam masala
½ tsp ground coriander
1 tsp chaat masala

**FRIED ONION RINGS**

2–3 tbsp vegetable oil
2 onions, peeled and cut into rings
3 tbsp tomato purée
sea salt and freshly ground black pepper
1 tsp garam masala
½ tsp chaat masala
handful of coriander leaves, to garnish

# Sweet potatoes with panch phoran

**SERVES 4**

2 medium sweet
  potatoes
2 tbsp vegetable oil
1 tbsp ghee or melted
  unsalted butter
2 tbsp chopped
  coriander and 1 tbsp
  ginger, peeled and cut
  into matchsticks
  (optional), to garnish

**PANCH PHORAN**

1 tsp nigella or black
  onion seeds
1 tsp fennel seeds
1 tsp fenugreek seeds
1 tsp cumin seeds
1 tsp black mustard
  seeds

You can buy a ready-made packet of panch phoran (an equal blend of five dried spices that is popular in Bengal) quite easily at Asian grocers. If, like me, you've already got a good selection of different spices in your kitchen cupboard, you may want to mix the blend yourself. I've listed the spices here should you choose to do so, but I would also suggest making up a large batch for storing so that you'll always have it to hand.

First, combine all the spices for the panch phoran and set aside. Peel the sweet potatoes and cut into 2cm dice. Blanch them in boiling salted water for 5 minutes, then drain well.

Heat the oil in a wide sauté pan. Add the panch phoran, and when the seeds start to crackle and pop, add the sweet potatoes. Stir well and sauté until the sweet potatoes are cooked through and browning slightly around the edges. Add the ghee or butter to the pan, and when it has been absorbed by the sweet potatoes, remove the pan from the heat.

Tip the potatoes into a warm serving bowl and sprinkle with chopped coriander and strips of ginger, if you wish.

# Stir-fried butternut squash with dried chilli

I love the unfussiness of this dish and the fact that you can make a delicious plate of food with a handful of ingredients. Butternut squash is fantastic cooked this way, but the simple spicing would also work well with sweet potatoes, yam and pumpkin.

Peel the butternut squash, discard the seeds and cut into 2cm cubes. Blanch in boiling salted water for 5 minutes then drain well.

Heat the oil in a wide sauté pan. Add the cumin and onion seeds and fry for 30 seconds, then add the garlic. Sauté gently for a couple of minutes until the garlic is soft but not coloured.

Add the butternut squash and chillies to the pan and toss well to coat with the spices. Season well and cook for a further 4–6 minutes, until the butternut-squash pieces are tender and beginning to crisp slightly around the edges. Serve piping hot as part of a main meal.

**SERVES 4**

1 large butternut squash
2 tbsp vegetable oil
1 tsp cumin seeds
1 tsp onion seeds
2 garlic cloves, peeled and finely chopped
3–4 dried red chillies, deseeded and chopped
sea salt and freshly ground black pepper

# Spicy cucumber and coconut salad

**SERVES 4**

1 large cucumber
1 green or red chilli, deseeded and finely chopped
3 tbsp freshly grated (or toasted desiccated) coconut
2 tbsp lemon juice, or to taste
1 tbsp chopped coriander
2 tbsp salted peanuts, lightly crushed
1 tbsp vegetable oil
1 tsp mustard seeds
4–5 curry leaves
pinch of asafoetida (optional)

This refreshing South Indian-style salad serves as a great accompaniment to any number of hot, fiery dishes. I also like to offer it alongside Indian starters, of which many are brown and deep-fried, to provide a hit of freshness and colour.

Peel the cucumber, cut it in half lengthways and scoop out the seeds using a spoon. Cut the flesh in half horizontally and then into long, thin strips using a swivel peeler or mandolin. Put the cucumber into a bowl and mix together with the chilli, coconut, lemon juice, coriander and peanuts.

Heat the oil in a pan and add the mustard seeds, curry leaves and asafoetida, if using. When they become fragrant (it should take less than a minute), remove from the heat and scatter over the salad. Mix well and serve.

# Breads & rice

Goan mussel pilau

Puri

Tamarind or 'Festival' rice

Coconut rice

Coriander puris with chickpea masala

Vegetable pilau

Pilau rice with meatballs

Dum ba biryani

Chapattis

Parathas

Jeera rice

Chicken biryani

Naan

Peshwari naan

Plain dosa

# Goan mussel pilau

SERVES 4

250g basmati rice

700g mussels, washed
and debearded

2 onions, peeled and
roughly chopped

4 garlic cloves, peeled
and roughly chopped

3cm ginger, peeled and
roughly chopped

1 green chilli, deseeded
and roughly chopped

2 tbsp coconut or
vegetable oil

about 400ml water

1½ tbsp ghee or melted
unsalted butter

2 cloves

2 cardamom pods

1 bay leaf

1 tsp ground coriander

½ tsp ground turmeric

75g finely grated fresh
coconut

sea salt and freshly
ground black pepper

Although small in size, the state of Goa is a major culinary force in India, and it has a unique cuisine due to a strong Portuguese influence. Goan cooking relies heavily on fresh and dried spices, coconut and fresh fish. In fact, a large majority of the population will eat some type of seafood at least once a day. This dish is a fine example of how fresh mussels can lend fantastic flavours to mildly spiced aromatic rice.

Wash the rice in several changes of cold water then leave to soak for 30 minutes in fresh cold water. Meanwhile, wash the mussels well and discard any that are broken or do not open when lightly tapped on a work surface. Put the onions, garlic, ginger and green chilli in a food processor with 2 tablespoons of water and blend to a fine paste. Heat the oil in a large, heavy-based pan. Add the paste and cook for 4–5 minutes. Add 100ml of the water and bring to the boil. Tip in the mussels, cover with a lid and shake. Allow the mussels to steam for 4–6 minutes or until they have opened. Strain them through a colander and reserve the liquor. Discard any that have not opened.

Heat the ghee or butter in another wide, heavy-based pan. Add the cloves, cardamom, bay leaf, coriander and turmeric and fry for a minute or until the spices become fragrant. Tip in the drained rice and coconut and stir well to mix. Add enough water to the strained mussel liquor to make 625ml, then add to the pan, season to taste and bring to the boil. Reduce the heat, cover the pan with a lid and simmer for about 10 minutes, until the rice has absorbed most of the liquid. Take the pan off the heat, leaving the lid on, and let the rice steam for another 5 minutes. Fluff the rice with a fork and top with the mussels or lightly fold them through. Serve immediately.

# Puri

These delicious puffed-up breads are often eaten for breakfast in northern India, and they are great served with lentil dal or a curry with a thick sauce. Puris are best eaten freshly cooked, but you can prepare the dough in advance and keep it covered in cling film to prevent it drying out. When ready to cook, heat the temperature of the oil until it is hot enough that each round of dough blisters and puffs up almost instantly. Serve immediately, as puris tend to deflate with time.

Sift the flour and salt into a large bowl. Add the ghee or butter and combine with your hands until the mixture resembles breadcrumbs. Add the warm water, a little at a time (you may not need all of it), until you get a stiff ball of dough. Tip the dough out on to a lightly floured surface and knead for 10 minutes or until smooth and well combined. Wrap the dough in cling film and set aside to rest for 30 minutes. Knead the dough once more on a lightly oiled surface. (Do not dust the dough with flour as the flour will burn easily when deep-frying.) Divide into 12 balls and roll out each ball into a thin round – about 10–12cm in diameter. Keep the dough rounds covered with cling film on a tray, in a single layer, until you are ready to cook them.

Heat 3cm of oil in a wide, deep frying pan (or a deep-fryer) to 180–190°C – to test the temperature, drop a piece of dough in the oil and it should brown in 10–15 seconds. Gently lower each round into the hot oil, one at a time. Initially it will sink to the bottom of the pan before blistering or puffing up and rising to the surface. When the bottom side is a light golden brown, after 1–2 minutes, turn it over to cook the other side for 10–20 seconds. Drain the puri on a tray lined with kitchen paper and cook the rest. Serve while still hot.

**MAKES 12**
200g atta or chapatti flour, plus extra to dust
½ tsp fine sea salt
2 tbsp ghee or melted unsalted butter
100–125ml warm water
vegetable oil, for deep-frying and greasing

**SERVES 6**

400g basmati rice
½ tsp fenugreek seeds
½ cinnamon stick
1 tsp black peppercorns
1 tsp cumin seeds
2 tsp coriander seeds
6 dried red chillies
4 tbsp coconut or
  vegetable oil
1 tsp mustard seeds
½ tsp urad dal
1 tsp channa dal
6 curry leaves
1 tbsp white sesame
  seeds
1 tbsp skinned peanuts
700ml water
1 tsp sea salt, or to taste
2 tbsp tamarind paste
15g jaggery, grated
75g freshly grated
  coconut
3 tbsp sesame oil

# Tamarind or 'Festival' rice

Southern Indians love the distinct tanginess of tamarind rice, and it is immensely popular in Andhra Pradesh, Karnataka and Tamil Nadu (where locals refer to it as *pulihora*, *puliogare* or *puliyodharai* respectively). Tamarind rice is sometimes called 'festival rice' because it is served during most festivals in southern India, and it is generally cooked for worshippers to Hindu temples. I was shown how to make this dish in an ashram kitchen by four dynamic ladies, all of whom were staunch vegans and keen to show me the benefits of their diet and lifestyle. Although they were unsuccessful in converting me, I was truly impressed with the time, effort and detail that went into making every element of the tamarind rice. Admittedly, I have not been a fan of vegan food in the past, but this is one dish that I will make time and again.

Wash the rice in several changes of cold water then leave to soak for 30 minutes in fresh cold water. Drain well.

Place a dry frying pan over a medium heat. Tip in the fenugreek, cinnamon, black peppercorns, cumin, coriander and 4 dried chillies. Toast the spices for a minute, tossing them frequently, until they smell fragrant and are lightly golden brown. Tip them into a bowl and leave to cool, then grind to a fine powder using a spice grinder or pestle and mortar.

Roughly chop the remaining 2 dried red chillies. Heat the oil in a large frying pan and add the mustard seeds, urad and channa dals and chopped chillies. After 1 minute, or when the dals turn a golden-brown colour, stir in the curry leaves, sesame seeds and peanuts and roast carefully for 30 seconds. Add the drained rice to the pan and stir well to coat the grains in the spices. Pour in the water, add the salt and bring to the boil. Reduce the heat, cover the pan and simmer for 10 minutes until the most of the liquid has been absorbed. Turn off the heat and let the rice steam for 5 minutes.

While the rice is cooking, put the tamarind paste and 2–3 tablespoons of water into a small saucepan and stir well. Simmer for 3–4 minutes until the tamarind has reduced slightly. Stir in the jaggery until it dissolves then add a pinch of salt and the roasted ground spices. Take the pan off the heat.

Place a small frying pan over a medium heat, add the coconut and toast it, stirring frequently, until golden brown and fragrant.

When the rice is cooked, remove the pan from the heat and fold through the jaggery spice mix, roasted coconut and sesame oil. Serve hot.

# Coconut rice

This rice is popular in the coastal regions of India, particularly in areas such as Goa and Kerala, where fresh coconut is plentiful. The rice is lovely served with vegetable, seafood or chicken dishes, especially those cooked with coconut milk. It really pays to use freshly grated coconut, as desiccated coconut is too dry for this dish. You can either grate the coconut flesh yourself (see page 26), or buy a pack of frozen grated coconut from your local Indian grocer.

Wash the rice in several changes of cold water and then leave to soak for 30 minutes in fresh cold water. Drain well and put the rice into a pot with the water and a good pinch of salt. Bring to the boil, reduce the heat to a simmer and put a lid on the pot. Simmer gently for about 10 minutes until the rice is almost cooked through and all the water has been absorbed. Turn off the heat, leaving the lid on, and let the rice steam for another 5 minutes. Uncover and fluff the rice with a fork to separate the grains.

Heat the oil in a heavy-based pan and add the mustard seeds, cinnamon, cardamom and cloves. Fry over a medium-to-high heat until the seeds begin to pop. Stir in the coconut and fry for a minute. Add the rice and stir well for a few minutes until evenly combined and the rice has warmed through. Taste and season as necessary. Remove the pan from the heat and cover with a lid to keep warm.

Put the ghee or butter into a small pan and, when hot, add the curry leaves. Fry the leaves until fragrant and crisp then tip the ghee and leaves over the coconut rice. Add the coriander leaves and stir well to mix. Serve while still hot.

**SERVES 4**

200g basmati rice
350ml water
sea salt and freshly
  ground black pepper
2 tbsp coconut or
  vegetable oil
2 tbsp black mustard
  seeds
1 cinnamon stick
3 cardamom pods
4 cloves
100g freshly grated
  coconut (thawed if
  frozen)
2 tbsp ghee or melted
  unsalted butter
8–10 curry leaves
small bunch coriander,
  leaves chopped

# Coriander puris with chickpea masala

This recipe is based on *chole masala*, a Punjabi dish that is usually eaten with Indian breads as an afternoon snack or included as part of a meal. The chole is made with dried chickpeas, an important protein-rich pulse that is an essential part of the diet of India's numerous vegetarians. You need to soak the dried chickpeas in lots of water overnight so that they'll have enough time to swell to a third of their size before cooking. If you don't have time to make the coriander puris, simply serve the dish with store-bought plain puris or chapattis.

Place the chickpeas in a saucepan and pour over enough cold water to cover. Bring to the boil, then simmer for about 2 hours until they are very tender.

Next, make the puri dough. Sift the flour and salt into a large bowl, then stir in the coriander. Make a well in the centre and add the butter and warm water, a little at a time (you may not need all of it), until it forms a stiff ball of dough. Tip the dough out on to a lightly floured surface and knead for 10 minutes until smooth. Wrap it in cling film and leave to rest for about 20 minutes.

For the chickpeas, heat the oil in a karahi or large wok over a medium heat. Add the onions and stir frequently for 6–8 minutes until they are golden brown. Add the chillies, ginger and garlic and fry for 3–4 minutes, then add the tomatoes. Cook until the tomatoes have softened, then stir in the cumin, turmeric and garam masala.

**SERVES 4–6**

**CHICKPEA MASALA**
200g dried chickpeas, soaked overnight, rinsed and drained
2 tbsp vegetable oil
2 medium onions, peeled and finely chopped
2 green chillies, deseeded and finely chopped
3cm ginger, peeled and finely grated
2 garlic cloves, peeled and finely chopped
4 tomatoes, skinned and roughly chopped
½ tsp ground cumin
½ tsp ground turmeric
1 tsp garam masala

**CORIANDER PURIS**
200g chapatti or atta flour, plus extra to dust
½ tsp fine sea salt
3 tbsp chopped coriander leaves and stems
2 tbsp melted unsalted butter
about 100–125ml warm water
vegetable oil, for deep-frying

Drain the cooked chickpeas and add to the pan. Stir well and pour in about 150ml of water. Bring to a simmer and cook for 25–30 minutes or until most of the water has been absorbed.

Knead the puri dough briefly again, then divide into 12 balls. Roll out each ball into a thin round on a lightly oiled surface and layer them between sheets of baking parchment to stop them sticking together.

Heat 6cm of oil in a deep pan (or a deep-fryer) until very hot, about 180–190°C. Gently lower the dough balls, one at a time, into the hot oil and cook in several batches. The dough will sink to the bottom before puffing up and rising. With a metal spoon or spatula, spoon the hot oil over the puris to encourage them to puff up and blister. As one side turns golden brown, flip over the puri and cook the other side for 10–20 seconds. Remove the puri with a slotted spoon and drain on a baking tray lined with kitchen paper. Repeat until all the puris are cooked.

Ladle the chickpea masala into warm bowls and serve hot with the freshly cooked coriander puris.

# Pilau rice with meatballs

SERVES 4
**PILAU RICE**
300g basmati rice
2 tbsp ghee or melted
  unsalted butter
1 tsp cumin seeds
4 cardamom pods
8 cloves
1 cinnamon stick
2 bay leaves
400ml water
1 tsp sea salt, or to taste

**MEATBALLS**
500g good-quality
  minced lamb
1 medium onion, peeled
  and finely chopped
2 garlic cloves, peeled
  and finely chopped
1 tsp garam masala
1 tsp ground cumin
½ tsp ground coriander
¼ tsp cayenne pepper
sea salt and freshly
  ground black pepper
2 tbsp chopped
  coriander leaves
3 tbsp natural yoghurt

It seems that every country in the world has a version of a meatball dish that is meant to be served with a starchy food such as rice or pasta. This aromatic rice and meatball recipe stems from a fusion of Persian and Indian cuisines. It is a delicious and warming meal and all you would need to serve alongside is a raita and a vegetable dish or light salad.

Wash the rice in several changes of cold water and then leave to soak for 30 minutes in fresh cold water. Drain well and set aside.

In a large bowl, mix together all the ingredients for the meatballs. Fry off a small ball of mixture to check the seasoning and adjust if necessary. With damp hands, divide the mixture into 12 equal-sized balls. Chill in the fridge for at least 30 minutes to allow them to firm up.

To make the sauce, put the garlic, ginger and tomatoes into a blender or food processor and blend to a fine wet paste. Tip the paste into a bowl and stir in the chilli powder, coriander, garam masala and the paprika. Set aside.

Heat a thin layer of oil in a large non-stick saucepan and carefully add the meatballs. Cook for 2–3 minutes until lightly browned on all sides. Remove from the pan and transfer to a warm plate. Add the bay leaves, cardamom pods and cinnamon stick to the same pan and cook for a minute, before stirring in the onion. Fry for 6–8 minutes until golden brown.

## SAUCE

4 garlic cloves, peeled and finely chopped
2.5cm ginger, peeled and finely chopped
6 medium tomatoes, skinned and chopped
1 tsp hot chilli powder, or to taste
½ tsp ground coriander
1 tsp garam masala
1 tsp paprika
2–3 tbsp vegetable oil
2 bay leaves
4 whole cardamom pods
1 cinnamon stick
½ medium onion, peeled and finely chopped
400ml water

Pour in the paste you made earlier and cook over a medium heat for 8–10 minutes, stirring frequently. Add half the water to the pan and simmer until all the liquid has evaporated. Pour in the remaining water and bring to the boil. Gently return the meatballs to the pan, cover with a lid and cook over a low heat for 25–30 minutes. The dish is ready when the meatballs are nicely browned and the sauce is clinging to them.

Meanwhile, cook the rice. Heat the ghee or butter in a large pan. Add the cumin seeds, cardamom pods, cloves, cinnamon and bay leaves. Fry for a minute or until the spices become very fragrant. Add the drained rice to the pan and stir well to coat it in the ghee and spices. Pour in the water and salt and bring to the boil. Reduce the heat, cover the pan with a lid and simmer for 10 minutes, until the rice is cooked through. Remove the pan from the heat and let stand for another 5 minutes.

To serve, spoon the rice into one large (or individual) serving plate(s) and top with the meatballs and sauce.

# Dum ba biryani

The word *dum* in this biryani refers to a traditional method of steaming parboiled rice and marinated meat in a dough-sealed vessel. The finished biryani is brought to the table where the pastry is broken to release the wonderful aromas from the mixture of spice, rice and meat. This particular dish is based on the intricate *dum ba biryani* that I tried in Lucknow, which involved saffron-marinated quails' eggs, whole quails, chickens and goats all set on a bed of aromatic rice – an extravagant dish fit for kings! Although simplified, this recipe is still quite elaborate, but it certainly makes a grand celebratory dish for a special occasion.

First, wash the basmati rice in several changes of cold water, then leave to soak in a bowl of fresh cold water for at least 30 minutes.

Next prepare the stuffed chicken. In a small bowl, stir the saffron strands into the hot water with a pinch of salt and leave to infuse for a few minutes. Peel the quails' eggs, place in a small bowl and spoon over the saffron-infused water. Leave to soak for about 15–20 minutes, turning over a few times so that the eggs get evenly stained with the saffron colour.

In a wide bowl, stir together 1 teaspoon of salt, ½ teaspoon of pepper, 2 teaspoons of garam masala, 1½ teaspoons of chilli powder, the garlic, ginger and yoghurt. Add the boned chicken and spread the yoghurt mixture all over it. Leave to marinate for a few minutes.

**SERVES 6**
**AROMATIC RICE**
400g basmati rice
2 tbsp ghee or unsalted
  butter
1 cinnamon stick
5 cloves
2 bay leaves
4 cardamom pods
475ml water
150ml single cream
1 tbsp rosewater

**STUFFED CHICKEN**
pinch of saffron strands
3–4 tbsp hot water
sea salt and freshly
  ground black pepper
6 quails' eggs, hard-
  boiled for 2 minutes
3 tsp garam masala
2 tsp hot chilli powder
3 garlic cloves, peeled
  and finely crushed
3cm ginger, peeled and
  finely grated
350ml natural yoghurt
1 small whole chicken,
  about 1.4kg, boned and
  butterflied (get your
  butcher to do this)

**STUFFED CHICKEN (CONT.)**
2 tbsp vegetable oil
1 tsp cumin seeds
1 onion, peeled and
 finely chopped
2 garlic cloves, peeled
 and finely crushed
½ tsp ground turmeric
500g good-quality
 minced lamb
400g tin chopped
 tomatoes
150ml water

**BASIC DOUGH
(FOR SEALING)**
75g plain flour
4 tbsp water

**TO GARNISH**
handful of coriander
 leaves
30g toasted pine nuts
30g dried apricots,
 sliced

Heat a tablespoon of oil in a large frying pan. Add the cumin seeds and roast carefully for a minute. Stir in the onion and garlic and sauté gently for 4–6 minutes until the onion is softened but not coloured. Add the remaining 1 teaspoon of garam masala and ½ teaspoon of chilli powder and the turmeric and fry for a further minute before removing the pan from the heat. Allow the mixture to cool completely.

Preheat the oven to 200°C/Fan 180°C/Gas 6. Tip the mince into a large bowl, add the cooked onions and spices and season well with salt and pepper. Mix well to combine, using your hands if easier. Lay out the chicken, skin-side down, on a board and spread about three-quarters of the mince mixture on top, leaving a 2cm rim around the borders. Dot the saffron quails' eggs along the length of the chicken then roll up the chicken tightly and secure with kitchen string.

Place the chicken on a lightly oiled roasting tin and spread over any remaining yoghurt marinade from the bowl. Roast for about 1 hour– 1 hour and 20 minutes until just cooked through. To check, the juices should run clear when a skewer is inserted into the thickest part of the bird. Remove and allow to cool slightly.

While the chicken is roasting, shape the remaining mince mixture into meatballs, about the size of ping-pong balls. Heat a tablespoon of oil in a frying pan and when hot add the meatballs and cook for 2–3 minutes on each side until lightly browned all over. Remove the meatballs from the pan, set aside, and add the tomatoes. Cook for 2–3 minutes before pouring over the water to form a sauce. Bring to the boil and then remove the pan from the heat.

Drain the rice. Heat the ghee or butter in a large pot and fry the cinnamon, cloves, bay leaves and cardamom for about 30 seconds until fragrant. Add the rice and stir well to coat in the ghee or butter and spices. Pour in the water and bring to the boil. Reduce the heat, cover and simmer for 10 minutes. Meanwhile, mix the cream with the rosewater and a pinch of salt and stir well.

Find a large ovenproof casserole (with lid) in which you are happy to serve the dish. Spread the meatballs over the base of the dish and pour over the sauce. Spoon a third of the rice over the top, then sprinkle over a third of the rosewater cream. Place the roast stuffed chicken over the bed of rice then spoon the remaining rice around the chicken. Spoon the remaining rosewater cream over the rice then cover the pan with a lid.

Preheat the oven back to 200°C/Fan 180°C/Gas 6. For the basic dough, mix the flour with just enough water to form a firm dough. Roll the dough out into a long, thin strip then press the strip of dough around the wetted rim of the pan to seal the lid to the pan. Place the casserole in the oven for 30–35 minutes. Turn off the oven and allow the biryani to stand in the oven for 10 minutes before bringing it to the table. Break the pastry seal, remove the lid and scatter over the garnish of coriander leaves, pine nuts and apricots before serving.

# Chapattis

MAKES 12
250g atta or chapatti
  flour, plus extra to dust
1 tsp fine sea salt
150–200ml water

Chapattis (or *rotis*) are the staple food of northern India, where wheat is the main crop, and they appear in practically every meal. During my first few days in New Delhi, I felt quite inadequate at mealtimes as I watched fellow diners adeptly use small pieces of chapatti to scoop up a curry or dal. A chapatti is often referred to as a 'third hand' for this reason. In India, chapattis are cooked on a *tava*, a cast-iron flat plate that keeps a consistently hot temperature, but a cast-iron frying or griddle pan works just as well.

Sift the flour and salt into a large mixing bowl. Make a well in the centre and gradually add the water (you may not need all of it) and stir until the flour comes together to form a soft, cohesive dough. Tip the dough out on to a lightly floured surface and knead well until it forms a smooth ball. This should take about 8–10 minutes. Cover the dough with a damp tea towel and leave to rest for 30 minutes.

Lightly flour the work surface and your hands. Divide the dough into 12 equal-sized balls. Work with one ball of dough at a time (and keep the rest covered to prevent them drying out). Flatten the ball with your hands and then roll out to form a thin disc, about 12–15cm in diameter. Shake off the excess flour.

Heat a cast-iron frying pan or flat griddle over a medium heat. Lay the chapatti in the pan and cook for 1–2 minutes. When bubbles begin to form, flip it over and cook on the other side for a minute. To get it to puff up, hold it over a low open flame with tongs. When both sides are brown speckled, it is done. Remove and keep warm, covered with a clean tea towel, while you cook the rest. Serve immediately.

# Parathas

**MAKES 12**

175g atta or chapatti
   flour

150g plain flour, plus
   extra to dust

1 tsp fine sea salt

about 200g ghee or
   melted unsalted butter

175ml water

Parathas are made using similar dough to chapattis, except that they are enriched with ghee and folded into layers before cooking. These delicious layered breads hail from Peshawar, in Punjab, and they can be made into triangular or rectangular shapes, or stuffed with cooked vegetables or paneer and shaped into rounds. A stuffed paratha is usually eaten simply with ghee, some pickles and a raita, and this is considered an ideal, wholesome breakfast. Plain parathas often accompany thick spicy curries and are normally enjoyed with main meals. As with all Indian breads, they are best consumed hot from the pan.

Sift the two flours and salt into a large bowl. Add three-quarters of the ghee or butter, rubbing it into the flour with your hands until the mixture resembles breadcrumbs. Slowly add enough water to allow you to bring the mixture together into a ball (you may not need all of it).

Tip the dough out on to a floured surface and knead lightly for 8–10 minutes until the dough is smooth and soft. Put the dough in a lightly oiled bowl, cover with cling film and leave to rest for at least 30 minutes.

Divide the dough into 12 balls. Work with one ball at a time (and cover the others to prevent them drying out). Dust the ball and work surface lightly with flour and roll the dough out into a 15cm circle. Using a pastry brush, lightly brush the paratha with some of the remaining ghee or butter, then fold it to create a semi-circle. Brush again and fold in half to form a triangle. Roll out into a larger triangle, with sides approximately 18–20cm. (You could also shape the bread into rounds. Roll out a ball of dough into a rectangle, brush it with ghee and roll it up like a Swiss roll. Pull and roll it into a long, thin rope, then take one end of the rope and coil it around itself like a snake. Press down lightly with the palm of your hand and roll out into a thin circle.)

When you are ready to cook, place a wide cast-iron frying pan over a medium-to-low heat. Brush the pan lightly with a little more of the remaining ghee or butter and add the paratha. Cook for a minute then brush the upper surface with more oil before cooking the other side. When golden brown, remove the paratha from the pan. Keep warm while you cook the rest.

# Jeera rice

**SERVES 4–6**

300g basmati rice
2 tbsp ghee or melted
 unsalted butter
30g cashew nuts
1 tbsp cumin seeds
2 bay leaves
4 black peppercorns
1 cinnamon stick,
 broken in half
3 cloves
1 onion, peeled and
 finely sliced
400ml water
1 tsp sea salt, or to taste

This is a fragrant and tasty alternative to plain boiled rice. *Jeera* means cumin seeds in Hindi, and they give the rice a distinctive and warming fragrance and flavour. When gently roasted to a brown colour, the cumin seeds develop heady, nutty aromas that really enhance the flavour of a dish. This fragrant rice is a suitable foil for any type of vegetarian, meat or fish-based dish.

Wash the rice in several changes of cold water and then leave to soak for 30 minutes in fresh cold water.

Heat the ghee or butter in a heavy saucepan and add the cashew nuts. Fry for 3–4 minutes until golden brown and then remove the nuts from the pan with a slotted spoon. Set aside.

Add the cumin, bay leaves, peppercorns, cinnamon and cloves to the pan. Fry for a minute or until the spices begin to smell fragrant. Add the onion and sauté gently for 4–6 minutes until softened. Tip the drained rice into the pan and stir well to coat the rice in the spices and ghee.

Pour in the water, add the salt and bring to the boil. Reduce the heat, cover the pan with a lid and simmer for about 10 minutes, until the rice is almost cooked and most of the water has been absorbed. Turn off the heat and leave to stand, still covered, for another 5 minutes.

Fork through the rice to separate the grains and stir through the cashew nuts. Serve while still hot.

## SERVES 4
### CHICKEN

500g boneless and
   skinless chicken
   breasts, cut into
   bite-sized pieces
200ml natural yoghurt
1 tsp ground turmeric
1 tsp hot chilli powder
1 tsp garam masala
3cm knob of ginger,
   peeled and grated
3 garlic cloves, peeled
   and finely crushed
sea salt and freshly
   ground black pepper
1 tsp vegetable oil
2 tbsp ghee or melted
   unsalted butter
2 medium onions,
   peeled and finely
   sliced
1 cinnamon stick
5–6 cloves
3 cardamom pods

# Chicken biryani

A biryani is essentially a layered rice dish; it has Persian origins but has been adapted and incorporated into Moghlai cuisine. There are many biryani recipes available and the use of different spices and ingredients varies from region to region. Authentic biryani recipes generally require quite a few steps – none of which is at all difficult – but the end result truly justifies the time spent. This dish is fantastic for a weekend lunch, and any leftovers taste just as good the next day.

Place the chicken in a bowl with the yoghurt, turmeric, chilli powder, garam masala and half the ginger and garlic. Season with a pinch of salt and pepper and mix well to coat the chicken pieces evenly. Cover the bowl with cling film and marinate in the fridge for at least 30 minutes.

Heat the oil and one tablespoon of ghee or butter in a heavy-based pan and fry the onions, stirring frequently, over a medium heat for about 8–10 minutes until they soften and brown. Remove from the pan with a slotted spoon, squeezing out any excess oil first. Set aside.

Add the remaining ghee or butter to the pan and tip in the cinnamon, cloves and cardamom. Fry for 30 seconds until fragrant. Add the remaining garlic and ginger and cook for another minute. Add the chicken and marinade to the pan and stir well. Simmer for about 10 minutes over a medium heat, stirring occasionally, until the chicken is cooked through.

For the rice, heat another heavy-based pan until hot, then add the ghee or butter, cinnamon, star anise and cardamom. Fry for about 30 seconds until the spices smell aromatic. Tip in the rice and raisins and stir well to coat. Toast the rice over a medium heat for a minute, then add the water and a good pinch of salt. Bring to the boil then gently simmer. Cover with a lid and cook for about 8–10 minutes.

Remove the lid and spoon over the chicken pieces and sauce. Re-cover and simmer for another 5 minutes until the rice is ready. Take the pan off the hob and let it stand for 5 minutes with the lid on.

Transfer the biryani to a warm serving dish, mixing the chicken through the rice, then garnish with the fried onions and coriander leaves. Serve immediately.

**RICE**
2 tbsp ghee or melted unsalted butter
1 cinnamon stick
1 star anise
4 cardamom pods
300g basmati rice, rinsed and drained
85g raisins
375ml water
handful of coriander leaves, to garnish

# Naan

**MAKES 8**

150–175ml tepid milk
1 tsp caster sugar
1 tbsp dried yeast
450g plain flour
½ tsp fine sea salt
1 tsp baking powder
2 tbsp natural yoghurt
2 tbsp ghee or melted
 unsalted butter, plus
 extra for brushing
 (optional)
poppy, sesame or black
 onion seeds, for
 sprinkling (optional)

This classic bread has become so popular in the UK that most supermarkets sell it ready to reheat. To my mind, these are no match for homemade ones, not least because the varieties sold by supermarkets tend to be thick and doughy, resembling a blend of Indian and Western bread. Naans are traditionally cooked in an authentic tandoor, although you can achieve a good result in a domestic oven.

Pour the milk into a bowl, sprinkle in a teaspoon of sugar and the yeast and stir well. Set aside for 20 minutes until it becomes frothy.

Sift the flour, salt and baking powder into a large bowl. Add the yoghurt, ghee or butter, and yeast mixture and bring everything together to form a soft ball of dough. Tip the dough out on to a lightly floured surface and knead for 10 minutes or until smooth. Place the dough in a large lightly oiled bowl and cover with a damp tea towel or cling film. Leave to rise in a warm place for an hour or until the dough has doubled in size.

Preheat the oven to 220°C/Fan 200°C/Gas 7. Put two large, heavy baking trays in the oven. Divide the dough into eight balls. Work with one ball at a time and keep the rest covered with cling film to prevent them drying out. Flatten the ball with the palm of your hand, roll out to a 5mm round and then pull one side to form a teardrop shape. Gently prick all over with a fork. Sprinkle the naan with your chosen topping, if using, and gently press it into the dough. Transfer to the hot baking trays. Bake for 4–5 minutes until they have puffed up slightly and brown spots appear on the surface of the bread. If you wish, brush with some ghee or butter and serve hot.

# Peshwari naan

These stuffed naans are one of my favourite Indian breads. I love the slight sweetness that you get from the raisins and coconut. They only require a few additional minutes to make once you've prepared the basic naan dough, and they are so worth the extra effort.

Make up the naan dough and leave to rest. To make the filling, pulse the almonds, raisins, caster sugar and coconut in a food processor to get a coarse powder.

Preheat the oven to 220°C/Fan 200°C/Gas 7. Put two large, heavy baking trays in the oven. Divide and roll the dough out into eight 5mm rounds and sprinkle half of each one with some filling, leaving a 1cm border around the edge. Fold the other half of the round over the filling to enclose it, and then roll out the dough into a teardrop or oval shape.

Bake for 4–5 minutes until they have puffed up slightly and brown spots appear on the surface of the bread. If you wish, brush with some ghee or butter and serve hot.

**MAKES 8**

1 quantity of naan
  dough (as page 192)
75g blanched almonds
30g raisins
2 tbsp caster sugar
30g coconut, freshly
  grated
ghee or melted unsalted
  butter, to brush
  (optional)

**MAKES 6–7 LARGE
OR 12–14 SMALL**

250g basmati rice
100g urad dal
1 tsp fine sea salt, plus
 extra for seasoning
300ml warm water
2–3 tbsp vegetable oil
 or ghee

**POTATO AND ONION
STUFFING (OPTIONAL)**

2 large potatoes, about
 500g
2 tbsp vegetable oil
1 tsp mustard seeds
4 curry leaves, chopped
1 onion, peeled and
 finely chopped
1–2 green chillies, to
 taste, deseeded and
 finely chopped
½ tsp ground turmeric

# Plain dosa

Dosas originate from southern India, and they are essentially thin and crisp pancakes made from a mixture of fermented rice and lentils. They are often eaten plain with a pickle or chutney or with a fish, potato or lentil-based curry, depending on the region in which they are served. In Karnataka, spicy potato-and-onion-stuffed dosas (called *masala dosa*) are the local speciality, but many variations exist. I've given a simple recipe for this here if you wish to try it. For best flavour, you need to start this recipe two days ahead of serving.

Put the rice and urad dal into a large bowl and rinse with several changes of water, then add plenty of fresh water to cover and leave to soak overnight.

Drain the rice well and place the rice and lentils in a blender or food processor with the salt and 1 tablespoon of warm water. Blend, then, with the motor running, trickle in the rest of the water to form a thin smooth batter. (It is important to blend the rice and lentils finely at this stage.) Transfer the batter to a bowl, cover and leave in a warm spot for at least six hours or preferably overnight.

The next day, place a lightly oiled, non-stick frying pan over a medium –low heat and pour in a thin layer of batter, swirling the pan to coat or spreading it out with the back of a ladle. Cook the batter for about 50–60 seconds until it is set at the base and lightly golden, then flip over to cook the other side for the same amount of time. (If the batter is quite thick and difficult to spread, add a little extra water and stir well.) Transfer to a plate and keep warm in a low oven while you cook the rest.

If you want to make the potato and onion stuffing, peel and dice the potatoes into 2cm cubes. Blanch them in a pan of boiling salted water for about 5 minutes until tender. Drain well.

Heat the oil in a large frying pan over a medium heat. Add the mustard seeds and curry leaves and cook for a minute or until the seeds begin to pop. Add the onion and cook for 5–7 minutes, stirring occasionally, until soft and golden brown. Stir in the green chillies, turmeric and blanched potatoes and season to taste. Cook for a further 3–4 minutes until everything is heated through.

To serve, place a large spoonful of the masala filling in the middle of each freshly cooked dosa and roll up or fold into triangle shapes. Serve immediately.

# Chutneys & accompaniments

# Tadka dal

A simple everyday lentil dish that comes from the north of India. *Tadka* actually refers to the tempering of spices and flavourings before they are combined with the main ingredients, which in this case are yellow split peas. The dal is delicious with Indian flat breads or any rice dish. I especially enjoy it with Jeera rice (see page 186).

Tip the split peas into a saucepan and cover with the water. Add the turmeric, coriander, garam masala and curry leaves. Stir well and bring to the boil. Skim off any scum that rises to the surface and reduce the heat. Simmer for 30–40 minutes or until the lentils are tender. If the mixture becomes too dry, add a little more water.

Heat the oil in a pan over a medium heat. Add the cumin seeds and fry for a minute or until fragrant. Add the garlic and onion and fry for 4–6 minutes until lightly golden brown. Stir in the chilli powder and, after a minute, tip the chopped tomatoes into the pan. Season the mixture with salt and black pepper and simmer over a medium heat for 6–8 minutes.

Pour all the contents of the pan over the cooked lentils and stir well. Bring to a simmer and cook for a further 10–15 minutes until the lentils are soft and thick. If you prefer, add a little hot water to thin down the consistency. Taste and adjust the seasoning and serve hot.

**SERVES 4**

400g yellow split peas, rinsed well
1 litre water
½ tsp ground turmeric
½ tsp ground coriander
½ tsp garam masala
4 curry leaves
2 tbsp vegetable oil
1 tsp cumin seeds
2 garlic cloves, peeled and finely chopped
1 small onion, peeled and finely chopped
1½ tsp red chilli powder
4 medium tomatoes, skinned and finely chopped
sea salt and freshly ground black pepper

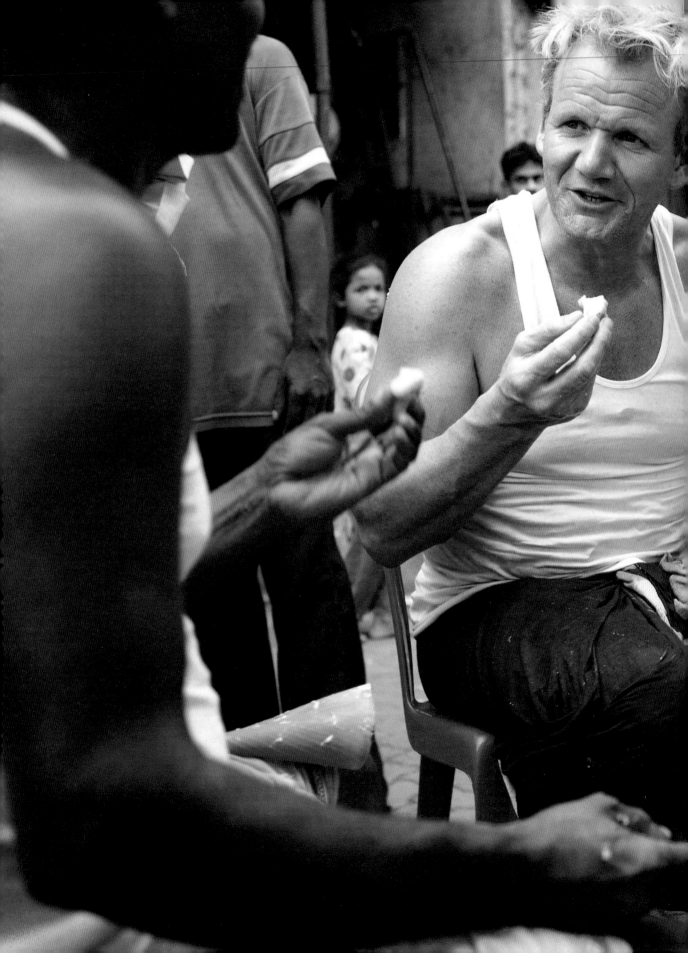

**SERVES 4–6**

500ml natural yoghurt
small bunch coriander,
  leaves picked
  and chopped
1 green or red chilli,
  deseeded and finely
  chopped
1 spring onion, trimmed
  and finely chopped
sea salt and freshly
  ground black pepper

# Coriander and chilli raita

Travelling through India, I was amazed at the variety of raitas served in every region. It was clear that there is no hard and fast rule when it comes to making a raita. It can be a thick and chunky dip with lots of vegetables and herbs, or resemble a light sauce that is highly seasoned with salt and spices. The only common denominator was the use of fresh yoghurt. This coriander and chilli raita is one of the easiest ones to whip up in minutes.

Whisk the yoghurt briefly in a bowl. Holding back a little chopped coriander and chilli to garnish, mix the rest with the yoghurt. Stir in the spring onion and seasoning to taste. Scatter the remaining chilli and coriander on top. Cover with cling film and chill, if not serving immediately.

# Green mango chutney

**MAKES ENOUGH TO FILL
A 350ML JAR**

500g unripe green
  mangoes
1 tbsp vegetable oil
1 tsp panch phoran
  (see page 154)
100ml white wine
  vinegar
100g caster sugar
  or jaggery
2.5cm ginger, peeled
  and very finely
  chopped
1–2 green chillies,
  deseeded and finely
  chopped, to taste
1 tsp sea salt

The Indians are very proud of their mangoes, which are unbelievably sweet and fragrant when ripe. I must also say that the Indians are also experts in making the best use of unripe green mangoes. Grated raw mangoes are often added to curries (to add a sour and fresh element) and made into spicy, sweet and sour chutneys to be served with all types of snacks, starters and flat breads. Traditionally, the ingredients for a chutney are all simply ground together and seasoned to taste, and it would need to be consumed on the same day it is made. I prefer to use this rather more 'Westernised' approach, where the ingredients are cooked with generous amounts of sugar and vinegar so that the resulting chutney can be kept for longer when properly stored.

Peel the mangoes, remove the stone and cut the flesh into 2cm cubes.

Heat the oil in a saucepan, add the panch phoran and fry for 1 minute or until the seeds begin to splutter and become fragrant. Add the vinegar and sugar and stir until the sugar has dissolved and the liquid has been absorbed. Add the mango, ginger, chillies and salt to the pan, stir well and cook over a low heat for 35–40 minutes until the mango is tender and sticky. Meanwhile, sterilise the storage jar by washing it well in warm soapy water, then dry it thoroughly in a low oven, about 100°C/Fan 80°C/Gas ¼, for 10–15 minutes.

Remove the pan from heat and cool slightly. While still hot, spoon the chutney into the sterilised jar and seal immediately with the lid. Let it cool completely, then keep the jar in the fridge and eat within a month.

# Red kidney bean dal

This is based on *dal makhani*, a Punjabi classic made with red kidney beans and black gram that is one of the better-known Indian dal dishes. In Hindi, *makhani* means 'with butter', and this is traditionally a rich, sumptuous and wholesome dish. For a lighter and healthier version, I've reduced the amount of butter and cream in this recipe, but do try not to leave them out completely as they help to blend the flavours of the dal and give it a creamy texture.

Drain the kidney beans and the urad dal and tip into a large saucepan. Pour in the fresh water to cover and add the ginger, ground coriander, chilli powder and turmeric. Bring to the boil and skim off any scum that rises to the surface, then reduce the heat and simmer for 30–40 minutes until the pulses are soft. When the pulses are cooked, remove the pan from the heat and mash lightly with a fork or potato masher, leaving some of the beans and dal whole.

Heat the oil in a frying pan over a medium heat, add the fennel and cumin seeds and roast carefully for a minute or until fragrant. Add the garlic, ginger and onion to the pan and cook for 6–8 minutes or until the onion is soft and golden brown. Tip the chopped tomatoes into the pan and cook for another 5–6 minutes until the tomatoes are very soft and the oil is beginning to separate from the ingredients.

Stir the beans and dal into the pan and add 200–300ml of water, enough to achieve a thin consistency. Bring to a simmer and cook over a low heat for 4–6 minutes, stirring frequently. Stir in the butter and cream and adjust the seasoning to taste. Simmer for another 2–3 minutes before serving hot, garnished with the coriander leaves.

**SERVES 4**

200g red kidney beans, soaked overnight in plenty of water
150g urad dal, soaked overnight in plenty of water
800ml water
3cm ginger, peeled and finely chopped
1 tsp ground coriander
1 tsp red chilli powder
1 tsp ground turmeric
2 tbsp vegetable oil
1 tsp fennel seeds
½ tsp cumin seeds
2 garlic cloves, peeled and finely chopped
2.5cm ginger, peeled and finely chopped
1 onion, peeled and finely chopped
4 tomatoes, skinned and chopped
1–2 tbsp unsalted butter, to taste
2–3 tbsp double cream, to taste
handful of coriander, leaves picked, to garnish

Serves ...

1 ... granate
500m... ...ral yoghurt
3 tbsp chopped mint
   leaves
sea salt and freshly
   ground black pepper
squeeze of lemon juice

# Pomegranate and
# mint raita

This pretty and refreshing raita is the perfect antidote
to hot and fiery curries. You can also substitute the
pomegranate seeds with half a cucumber that has
been peeled, deseeded and grated.

Place a frying pan over a medium heat; add the cumin seeds and roast
carefully for a minute or until the cumin begins to smell very
fragrant. Remove from the heat and allow to cool completely before
grinding the seeds to a powder in a pestle and mortar.

Roll the pomegranate on a hard surface, applying pressure with your
hands in order to loosen the seeds. Cut the pomegranate in half and
scrape the seeds out into a bowl. Try to avoid leaving on any of the
bitter white pith.

Whisk the yoghurt briefly in a small bowl then add most of the
chopped mint and pomegranate seeds, and the roasted cumin.
Season to taste with salt, black pepper and lemon juice and mix well.
Scatter over the remaining chopped mint and pomegranate seeds to
garnish. Serve immediately or chill for later consumption.

# Sambar

This is a thin vegetable stew flavoured with tamarind and thickened with tuvar dal, which is very popular in the southern regions, especially in Andhra Pradesh, Karnataka, Kerala and Tamil Nadu. Each region has a particular way of eating sambar, but it is almost always served with green coconut and tomato chutneys and either rice or an Indian flat bread, such as dosa. I had the honour of making my first sambar with Sambar Mani, who grew up in one of Mumbai's largest slums, and he now makes a good living catering for small and large events within the slums. Mani has had a lifelong love of cooking and his attention to detail shows in his food. His sambar was absolutely delicious, unlike any Indian vegetarian food I had tried previously in the UK. This recipe is my humble attempt at replicating the flavours of Mani's sambar.

Place a frying pan over a medium heat and carefully roast all the ingredients for the masala. When the spices begin to smell very fragrant and are nicely roasted, remove the pan from the heat and allow to cool completely. Use a spice grinder or pestle and mortar to grind the spices into a powder. Tip into a small bowl and add enough water, about 3–4 tablespoons, to form a thick paste with a slow-dropping consistency.

Put the tuvar dal and curry leaves into a medium saucepan and cover with 1½ litres of water. Bring to the boil and skim off any scum that rises to the surface. Reduce the heat slightly and leave to simmer for 25–30 minutes or until the lentils are tender. Drain and set aside.

SERVES 4–6
MASALA
2 tsp fenugreek seeds
1 tbsp yellow split peas
2 tsp coriander seeds
6 curry leaves
4 dried red chillies

SAMBAR
200g split pigeon pea lentils (tuvar dal)
6 curry leaves
100g tamarind pulp
2 tbsp vegetable oil
1 tsp mustard seeds
1 tsp fennel seeds
½ tsp cumin seeds
4 dried red chillies
1 medium aubergine, trimmed and cut into 2cm pieces
¼ butternut squash, peeled, deseeded and cut into 2cm pieces
3 medium carrots, peeled and cut into 2cm pieces

## SAMBAR (CONT.)

1 tsp ground turmeric
1 tsp sea salt, or to taste
50g okra, washed, dried
  and trimmed
4 tomatoes, skinned
  and finely chopped
1 tsp ground coriander
1 tsp red chilli powder
small bunch coriander,
  leaves picked and
  chopped
1 tbsp ghee or melted
  unsalted butter

Soak the tamarind in 200ml of hot water for 20 minutes; use your hands to break down the block into smaller pieces. Strain the mixture through a sieve and discard the husks and seeds.

Heat the vegetable oil in a large pan and add the mustard, fennel and cumin seeds and the dried chillies. Cook for 1 minute or until the spices become very fragrant. Add the aubergine, butternut squash and carrots, stirring well to coat the vegetables in the spices. After 2–3 minutes add the turmeric, salt and tamarind water to the pan and bring to the boil. Boil for 8–10 minutes or until the vegetables are tender but not mushy.

Add the okra, cooked lentils, ground masala spice, chopped tomatoes, ground coriander and chilli powder to the pan and stir well. Add more water to the pan if necessary. (The sambar should be quite thin in consistency.) Bring to the boil, then reduce the heat and leave to simmer for 5 minutes until the okra is just tender. Taste and adjust the seasoning.

Just before serving, stir through the chopped coriander and ghee or butter. Serve the sambar hot with freshly steamed rice and warm Indian breads.

# Spicy green chutney

This vibrant mint and coriander chutney is usually paired with tamarind chutney, as both are ideal, all-purpose condiments for fried Indian snacks. Both chutneys can also be used as a sauce to spoon over plain rice or grilled meats, fish and kebabs. I have left the quantities for the ingredients fairly loose, as you should treat the recipe as a guideline and add the raw garlic, chillies and seasoning according to taste. You could also add a tablespoon or two of grated fresh coconut to give the chutney a thicker texture and different flavour profile.

Except for the water, put all of the ingredients into a food processor. Blend to a smooth purée. With the motor still running, gradually pour in enough water until the chutney has a thin pouring consistency. Taste to check the seasoning and add more salt, sugar or lime juice, as you wish.

Transfer the chutney to a bowl, cover with cling film and chill, if not serving immediately. Store in the fridge and eat within 2–3 days.

**SERVES 6**

bunch mint leaves, about 25–30g, leaves roughly chopped
bunch coriander, about 25–30g, stems and leaves roughly chopped
1–2 small garlic cloves, peeled and finely chopped
1–2 green chillies, deseeded and roughly chopped
½ small onion, peeled and finely chopped
½ tsp sea salt, or to taste
½ tsp jaggery or light brown soft sugar, or to taste
juice of 1 lime, or to taste
100–150ml water

# Sweet tamarind chutney

This ubiquitous sweet-and-sour chutney comes from Bengal, and it frequently accompanies deep-fried starters or snacks such as bhajis, samosas and pakoras. This recipe is a simple no-cook one, which means that the chutney won't last long, and it will need to be consumed within a few days of making.

Soak the tamarind in the hot water for 20 minutes; using your hands break the block down into smaller pieces first. Once softened, strain the mixture through a fine sieve and discard the husks and seeds.

Place a frying pan over a medium heat and add the cumin and coriander seeds. Dry roast them for a minute, then tip the spices into a bowl.

Place the chilli powder, salt, jaggery or sugar and dates into a blender. Add the roasted cumin and coriander seeds and 2 tablespoons of water and blend to a fine purée. Scrape the purée into a bowl and mix in the tamarind extract. Stir well and add a little water if you think the chutney is too thick (it should have a thin pouring consistency). Cool completely, store in the fridge and eat within 3 days.

**MAKES ENOUGH TO FILL A 350ML JAR**
200g tamarind pulp
400ml hot water
1 tsp cumin seeds
1 tsp coriander seeds
1 tsp red chilli powder
1 tsp sea salt
100g jaggery or light brown soft sugar
30g dates, pitted

# Coconut chutney

**COCONUT CHUTNEY**
freshly grated flesh of
 1 coconut, about 250g
2 tbsp roasted channa
 dal
30g cashew nuts
2.5cm ginger, peeled
 and roughly chopped
small bunch coriander,
 leaves and stems
 roughly chopped
1 green chilli, deseeded
 and finely chopped
1 tbsp tamarind paste
1 tsp cumin seeds
½ tsp caster sugar
½–1 tsp sea salt, to taste
50–75ml water

**SPICES FOR TEMPERING**
2 tbsp vegetable oil
1 tsp mustard seeds
1 tsp cumin seeds
2 whole dried red
 chillies, halved
1 tsp urad dal
8 curry leaves
pinch of asafoetida
 (optional)

This chutney is a great accompaniment to South Indian breads, such as dosa and puri, and it is usually eaten as part of a breakfast spread. It is essential to use fresh coconut to get the best texture and flavour for the chutney, even though it may take a little time and effort to grate. I like to serve this with some store-bought crispy poppadoms as an instant snack.

Except for the water, put all the ingredients for the coconut chutney into a food processor. Blend to a fine wet paste, adding a little water and scraping down the sides of the bowl as necessary. Taste and check the seasoning then transfer the mixture to a bowl.

To temper the spices, heat the oil in a frying pan over a medium heat. Add the mustard seeds, cumin seeds, red chillies, urad dal, curry leaves and asafoetida, if using. Cook for 1–2 minutes, until the mustard seeds begin to pop and splutter and the mixture is fragrant. Remove the pan from the heat and immediately tip the oil and spices over the coconut paste. Stir well and transfer to a serving bowl or a clean kilner jar. The chutney is best served freshly made with warm Indian breads.

# Cholar dal

This is a lentil dish that is often served during festivities and special events, and it frequently graces the buffet spread at Indian weddings. It has a delicious hint of sweetness, from the addition of sugar or raisins, and is typically served with puris or plain chapattis.

Wash the soaked lentils in fresh water then drain and transfer to a saucepan. Pour the water into the pan and add the turmeric, cumin, garam masala, 1 teaspoon of sugar and the green chilli. Give the mixture a stir and bring to the boil then skim off any scum that rises to the surface. Reduce the heat to a simmer and cook for 35–40 minutes until the lentils are soft and thick.

Heat the ghee or butter in a heavy-based pan. Add the cumin seeds, cardamom pods, cinnamon and bay leaves and fry for 1–2 minutes until the spices become aromatic. Stir in the coconut and mild chilli powder, if using, and mix well. Cook for a further 2–3 minutes until lightly browned, then remove the pan from the heat.

Pour the ghee or butter and spices into the pan containing the lentils and stir to mix, seasoning to taste. Serve hot.

**SERVES 4–6**

250g channa dal, soaked in water for 4–6 hours
1 litre water
½ tsp ground turmeric
1 tsp ground cumin
1½ tsp garam masala
2 tsp caster sugar
1 green chilli, slit in half
2 tbsp ghee or melted unsalted butter
2 tsp cumin seeds
4 cardamom pods, lightly crushed
1 cinnamon stick
2 bay leaves
75g coconut, freshly grated
1 tsp mild chilli powder (optional)
sea salt, to taste

# Pineapple and raisin chutney

This Bengali chutney is excellent eaten with plain Indian flat breads or as an accompaniment to a main meal. It goes particularly well with poultry and game, and I would not think twice about serving it with a Western meal such as roast pork or gammon. Unlike for Green mango chutney (see page 206), I find it is better to use sweet, overripe pineapples when making this chutney.

Peel and core the pineapple and dice the flesh into 1cm cubes.

Heat 2 tablespoons of the oil in a large saucepan over a medium heat. Add the garlic and ginger and cook for 3–4 minutes until softened but not coloured. Tip the jaggery or brown sugar and the granulated sugar into the pan and cook for 2–3 minutes until the sugars caramelise.

Add the chillies, chilli powder, pineapple, raisins and water to the pan and stir well. Reduce the heat and simmer, stirring occasionally, for 30–40 minutes or until you get a thick jammy consistency.

Heat the remaining oil in a frying pan and add the panch phoran. When the seeds crackle and splutter, remove from the heat and add the roasted spices and oil to the chutney. Stir well and, while still hot, transfer to a sterilised jar (see page 206) and seal well. Store in the fridge and consume within a week.

**MAKES ENOUGH TO FILL A 350ML JAR**

1 medium ripe
  pineapple
3 tbsp vegetable oil
2 garlic cloves, peeled
  and finely chopped
2cm ginger, peeled and
  finely chopped
50g jaggery, grated, or
  light brown soft sugar
50g granulated sugar
2 dried red chillies,
  finely chopped
½ tsp red chilli powder
150g raisins
200ml water
1 tsp panch phoran
  (see page 154)
sea salt, to taste

**MAKES ENOUGH TO FILL
A 350ML JAR**

500g tomatoes
1 tbsp vegetable oil
1 tsp black onion seeds
4 curry leaves, roughly
 chopped
2 small onions, peeled
 and finely chopped
3cm ginger, peeled and
 finely chopped
100g caster sugar
200ml white wine
 vinegar
1 medium or ½ large
 cucumber, peeled and
 cut into fine dice
sea salt and freshly
 ground black pepper

# Tomato and cucumber chutney

This lovely sweet-and-sour chutney has a jammy consistency but with extra texture from the addition of diced cucumber. It is fantastic served with Indian starters and meals, but I'm also partial to spreading spoonfuls of it on ham sandwiches. It is also a great way to make use of the summer glut of tomatoes.

To skin the tomatoes, lightly score the top and bottom of each tomato with a sharp knife. Drop the tomatoes into a pan of simmering water and blanch them for 40–50 seconds. Remove them with a slotted spoon and drop into a bowl of iced water to cool. Drain and peel off the skins before chopping the flesh into rough dice.

Heat the oil in a large pan and add the onion seeds and curry leaves. Fry for a minute or until the seeds begin to pop and splutter. Add the onions and ginger and sauté gently for 3–4 minutes until the onions have softened slightly. Add the sugar and vinegar, increase the heat slightly and stir to help the sugar dissolve.

Add the diced tomatoes to the pan, reduce the heat and simmer gently for 35–40 minutes, stirring frequently, until all the liquid released by the tomatoes has been absorbed and the mixture is tacky. If the chutney seems too runny, cook for a further 10–15 minutes. Add the diced cucumber to the pan, stir well to combine and cook for 2–3 minutes. Remove the pan from the heat and taste to check the seasoning, adding a little more salt and pepper as necessary. While the chutney is still hot, spoon into a sterilised jar (see page 206) and seal tightly. Keep in the fridge and consume within a month.

**SERVES 4–6**
300g spinach leaves
1 tbsp vegetable oil
1½ tsp cumin seeds
1 tsp mustard seeds
500ml natural yoghurt
1 tsp chilli powder,
  or to taste
sea salt and freshly
  ground black pepper
squeeze of lemon juice

# Spinach raita

A great healthy yoghurt dish, this raita is best made
a few hours ahead of serving as it tastes better once
the flavours have had time to develop.

Bring a large pan of salted water to the boil, add the spinach and
blanch for a minute. Drain through a colander and refresh under cold
running water. With the spinach still in the colander, press down with
the back of a large spoon or ladle to squeeze out the excess moisture.
Pat the spinach dry with kitchen paper, then lay the leaves out on a
chopping board and chop finely.

Put the oil in a small frying pan and place over medium heat. Add
the cumin and mustard seeds and fry for a minute or until the seeds
begin to pop and splutter. Pour the oil and seeds into a small bowl
and leave to cool.

Whisk the yoghurt briefly in a large bowl, then add the chopped
spinach, roasted cumin and mustard seeds and chilli powder. Season
well with salt, black pepper and lemon juice and chill until you are
ready to serve.

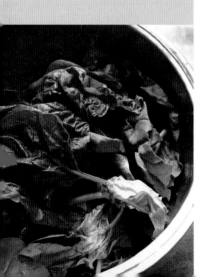

# Aubergine raita

**SERVES 4–6**
2 small aubergines
1 shallot or ½ onion,
  peeled and roughly
  chopped
1 small garlic clove,
  peeled and chopped
juice of ½ lemon,
  or to taste
1 tsp cumin seeds
500ml natural yoghurt
1 tsp red chilli powder,
  or to taste
sea salt and freshly
  ground black pepper

This is a great way to serve aubergines, and it reminds me of the Persian-style roasted aubergine dips that are popular throughout the Mediterranean countries. Eat it with poppadoms as a healthy snack or spoon on to chapattis and serve with Galouti or Paneer tikka kebabs (see pages 34 and 35).

Preheat the grill to high. Prick the aubergines all over with a fork and place under the grill for 6–8 minutes, turning occasionally, until the skin blisters all over. Place them in a large bowl and cover with cling film. Set aside for about 10 minutes.

When the aubergines are cool enough to handle, peel away the skins. Roughly dice the flesh then tip into a colander set over a bowl. Leave for 15 minutes to allow the moisture to drain away. Once drained, put the aubergine flesh in a food processor with the shallot or onion, garlic and lemon juice and blend to a fine purée.

Place a frying pan over a medium heat. Add the cumin seeds and dry roast for a minute or until the cumin smells very aromatic. Add the aubergine purée to the pan and cook over a medium–high heat for 4–6 minutes or until the mixture has thickened. Tip into a large bowl and allow to cool completely.

Add the yoghurt to the aubergine mixture and stir in the chilli powder and seasoning to taste. Cover the bowl with cling film and chill until ready to serve.

# Sweets & drinks

Coconut burfi

Fruit salad with spiced syrup

Mango porridge

Gulab sharbat

Ginger fruit punch

Sweet yoghurt with saffron, cardamom and
  pistachios

Mango and mint lassi

Salty lassi with ginger and cumin

Almond halwa

Masala chai

Lightly spiced sesame and cashew nut cookies

Payasam

Gulab jamon

Cardamom and coconut-flavoured milk

Rasmalai

Rosewater kulfi

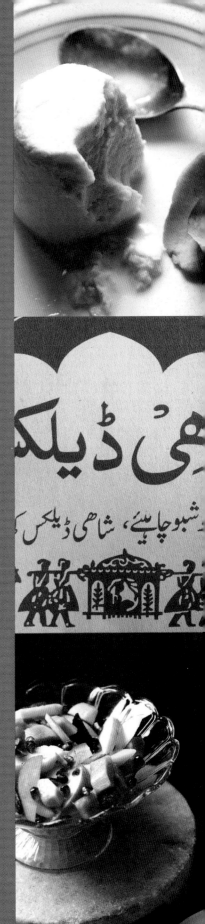

**SERVES 4–6**
200g freshly grated
coconut
100g desiccated coconut
100g caster sugar
400ml tin condensed
milk
4–5 cardamom pods,
seeds finely ground
4 tbsp unsalted butter,
plus extra to grease
handful of roasted and
skinned pistachio
nuts, finely chopped
(optional), to decorate

# Coconut burfi

I'm always amazed when I step into an Indian sweet shop and see the colourful array of sweetmeats lined up in neat rows behind glass counters. Invariably there will be at least a handful of different *burfis* (sometimes spelt *barfis*), made from fruits or nuts with lots of sugar and ghee. In India, some form of *halwa* or *burfi* is served during religious festivals and weddings. Coconut burfi is often eaten during Diwali, the festival of lights. They remind me of our old-fashioned fudge – rich and buttery but with a slightly crumbly texture and a subtle flavour of cardamom. These are sure to be popular with children.

Put the fresh coconut, desiccated coconut, sugar and condensed milk into a wide pan and place over a medium-to-low heat. Stir frequently for 20–25 minutes until the mixture has thickened to a fudge consistency. (Do not leave the pan unattended as the mixture should not take on any colour.) Stir in the ground cardamom and butter and remove the pan from the heat.

Tip the mixture into a lightly buttered baking dish and spread out to about a 2–3cm thickness. Leave to cool completely then chill for at least 30 minutes to allow the mixture to firm up.

Cut the coconut burfi into small diamonds or squares. If you wish, decorate each diamond or square with a little chopped pistachio to serve.

# Fruit salad with spiced syrup

As is the case in most of Asia, desserts do not feature prominently in Indian cuisine. Rather, platters of cut seasonal fruit are usually passed around the table after a meal as a refreshing way to cleanse the palate. The spiced syrup for this fruit salad is not authentic, but simply my way of lending some Indian flavours to a plate of mixed fruit. It goes without saying that you should use whatever fruit you like, provided it is nice and ripe.

First, make the spiced syrup. Put the sugar and water into a saucepan, place over a medium heat and stir to help the sugar dissolve. Add the black peppercorns, cinnamon, cardamom pods and lime zest. Bring to the boil briefly, then reduce the heat and simmer for about 10 minutes until the syrup has thickened slightly. Remove from the heat and leave to cool completely. If you wish, leave to infuse for several hours before using or straining into a jug.

When you are just about ready to serve, peel and thinly slice the mango, papaya and pineapple. Thinly slice the star fruits and apples, leaving the skin of the apples on, if you wish. Arrange the fruit in a large serving bowl (or individual bowls) and scatter over the pomegranate seeds. Drizzle over the spiced syrup and serve.

**SERVES 4**
1 large ripe mango
1 small ripe papaya
1 small ripe pineapple
2 star fruits
2 apples
seeds from
  ½ pomegranate

**SPICED SYRUP**
100g granulated sugar
150ml water
3 black peppercorns
1 small cinnamon stick
5 cardamom pods,
  lightly crushed
pared zest of 1 lime,
  cut into thin strips

# Mango porridge

**SERVES 4**

2 medium firm but ripe
  mangoes, peeled,
  stoned and diced
350ml coconut
  (or plain) water
350ml coconut milk
350ml whole milk
½ tsp sea salt
75g jaggery, grated (or
  light brown soft sugar)
1 tsp ground cinnamon,
  plus optional extra for
  dusting
50g freshly grated
  coconut
200g rolled oats
50g sultanas
30g toasted sliced
  almonds

Porridge does not spring to mind as an Indian sweet, but you'll be surprised to know (as I was) that rice porridge is often eaten by jockeys taking part in buffalo racing, a rural sport still popular in the coastal regions of southern India. The jockeys either ride on a wooden plank set behind pairs of buffaloes or run alongside the animals as they race down a muddy track. Either way, they need to maintain high energy levels, so before each race they consume bowls of porridge with many cups of chai (see page 253). Although not authentic, this oatmeal version was inspired partly by the race and partly by my Scottish roots. You can replace the oats with pudding rice, but that will need about 20 minutes to cook.

Tip half of the mango flesh into a blender or food processor and blend to a smooth purée. Set aside.

Pour the coconut or plain water, coconut and whole milks into a large pan. Bring to the boil over a medium heat. Stir in the salt, jaggery or sugar and cinnamon and boil for 2–3 minutes. Add the grated coconut and stir for a couple of minutes. Gradually add the oats to the pan and cook, stirring continuously, for about 4–6 minutes until the oats are plump and soft. If the pan seems too dry, add a little milk.

Just before you are ready to serve, stir in the sultanas and two-thirds of the mango purée. Spoon into individual bowls. Drizzle each one with the remaining mango purée and top with the rest of the chopped mango. Sprinkle over a little ground cinnamon, if you wish, and the toasted almonds and serve at once.

# Gulab sharbat

This delicate, refreshing and fragrant drink is excellent on a warm day. Gulab means 'rose', and this is made from rose syrup. You can buy bottles of rose syrup from Asian grocers, but these are generally made with artificial flavours and preservatives. It is not difficult to make your own, but you do need to get organic, edible roses with no trace of pesticide or other chemicals.

Put the rose petals into a large bowl and crush lightly with your hands. Pour over the boiling water, add the cardamom seeds and cover the bowl with cling film. Place in the fridge for at least 6 hours or overnight if possible.

Place a muslin-lined sieve over a saucepan and pour over the rose-infused liquid to strain out the rose petals and cardamom seeds. Put the pan over a low heat, add the sugar and stir continuously until the sugar has dissolved. Remove the pan from the heat and strain the liquid again into a bowl or jug. Add the lemon juice, pomegranate juice, water and rosewater to the mixture and stir well. Chill in the fridge for at least 30 minutes. Serve in chilled glasses.

**SERVES 4**
about 200 freshly picked rose petals, about 2 cups, plus extra to decorate
175ml boiling water
¼ tsp cardamom seeds
120g caster sugar
150ml lemon juice
450ml pomegranate juice
400ml cold water
1 tsp rosewater

# Ginger fruit punch

**SERVES 4**
15cm ginger, peeled and
  thinly sliced
200g caster sugar
100ml water
120ml fresh lemon juice
50ml fresh orange juice
cold water and lots of
  crushed ice, to serve

This tangy fruit punch is excellent served on a hot day or after a meal to help aid digestion. You will need a lot of fresh ginger to get a strong taste of gingery heat. As a rough guide, pick a young root that is about the size of the palm of your hand. Any leftover syrup can be stored in a sealed bottle and kept for 2–3 days.

Place the ginger, sugar and water in a small heavy-based saucepan over a medium heat. Bring to the boil and stir frequently to help the sugar dissolve. Add the lemon and orange juices, then reduce the heat and simmer gently for 15 minutes.

Remove the pan from the heat and leave the syrup to infuse for at least 30 minutes. Strain the liquid through a fine sieve into a jug and leave to cool before chilling in the fridge.

To serve, pour the ginger punch to fill a third of each serving glass, then top up with cold water and crushed ice.

# Sweet yoghurt with saffron, cardamom and pistachios

**SERVES 4**
1 litre thick Greek yoghurt
2 tbsp whole milk
generous pinch of saffron strands
150g icing sugar
2–3 cardamom pods, seeds finely ground
3 tbsp toasted pistachio nuts, roughly chopped

This is a very simple recipe that originates from western India. You can enjoy it plainly as a breakfast treat or dress it up with chopped nuts, caramelised orange slices and shredded mint leaves for an elegant dessert. For the latter, try substituting the cardamom with a little orange blossom water or rosewater. It is really worth leaving the yoghurt to hang in the fridge overnight so it becomes wonderfully creamy and dense.

Line a large sieve with muslin cloth or with several layers of kitchen paper and set it on top of a large bowl. Pour the yoghurt into the middle and leave to drain in the fridge for at least 4 hours or overnight. You can then pour off the drained whey in the bowl.

Warm the milk in a small pan (or in a small bowl in the microwave) and add the saffron strands. Remove the pan from the heat and leave to infuse for 20 minutes.

Tip the strained yoghurt into a bowl and sift in the icing sugar. Add the saffron milk, ground cardamom and 2 tablespoons of chopped pistachio nuts. Mix well and spoon into individual serving bowls or glasses. Chill, if not serving immediately.

Scatter the remaining chopped pistachios over the yoghurts just before serving.

# Mango and mint lassi

**SERVES 2**

1 large or 2 medium
  ripe mangoes
250ml Greek yoghurt
200ml whole or semi-
  skimmed milk
1 tbsp caster sugar,
  or to taste
few sprigs of mint,
  leaves stripped
  (optional), plus extra
  sprigs to decorate
handful of ice cubes
  (optional)

This Indian-style smoothie is filling and refreshing at the same time. When in season during the summer, do use fragrant Alphonso or Kesar mangoes to make the lassi. Truly ripe ones can be so sweet that you may not need to add extra sugar to the drink. Mangoes differ in size, so do taste and add sugar as you go along.

Peel the mango(es) and carefully remove the flesh from the stone. Place in a blender with the yoghurt, milk and sugar. If you wish, add a few mint leaves to the mixture. Blend until light and fluffy. Taste and add more sugar if you think that it is needed.

Pour the lassi into two tall, chilled serving glasses and add the ice cubes, if you wish. Decorate with mint sprigs and serve immediately.

# Salty lassi with ginger and cumin

Throughout Asia a little salt is added to cooling drinks as a way to quench thirst and replenish lost moisture during hot and humid days. This salty lassi is not only refreshing but also very tasty and satisfying. Enjoy it on its own or with a light meal.

Place a dry frying pan over a medium heat. Add the cumin seeds and roast gently until the seeds begin to smell very aromatic. Remove from the heat and allow to cool before grinding to a powder in a spice grinder or with a pestle and mortar.

Pour the yoghurt into a blender with the ginger, salt and cumin powder. Blend well. With the motor still running, gradually pour in the water until you are happy with the consistency. (Lassi is generally served quite thick, but feel free to thin it down, if you prefer.) Taste to see if more salt is needed. Pour the lassi into tall serving glasses and serve at once.

**SERVES 4**

1 tsp cumin seeds
350ml natural yoghurt
1.5cm ginger, peeled
  and finely chopped
¼ tsp sea salt, or to taste
200ml ice-cold water

**SERVES 6**
200g blanched almonds
100ml whole milk
pinch of saffron strands
150ml warm water
200g caster sugar
50g unsalted butter,
  diced, plus extra for
  greasing

# Almond halwa

*Halwas* are popular in northern India, particularly among Punjabi communities. They have Persian origins (in fact, many Arabic and Mediterranean cultures have their own form of *halwa*) and can be made using a whole host of different vegetables, fruits, nuts and spices. They are also served in various forms: from soft and wet puddings that you will need to consume with a spoon; to small, firm geometric shapes that you eat as candies. I prefer to serve them in the latter form to enjoy as petits fours.

Tip the almonds into a food processor, add the milk and blend to a thick paste. Crush the saffron strands to a fine powder using a pestle and mortar. Put the sugar, crushed saffron and the water into a saucepan over a medium heat. When the sugar has dissolved, increase the heat, bring the mixture to the boil and cook for 5 minutes. Add the almond paste to the pan and stir continuously to prevent any lumps forming. Stir frequently for 15–20 minutes until the mixture is very thick. (It will become quite difficult to stir.) Gradually add the butter and stir constantly over a low heat for another 4–6 minutes. The mixture should look shiny and slightly translucent.

Lightly butter a wide shallow dish. Remove the pan from the heat and scrape the mixture into the prepared dish. Use a palette knife to smooth and even out the mixture. Allow to cool completely before cutting into small squares or diamonds. You can also roll them into small round balls with your hands, once they have firmed up slightly in the fridge. Chill the halwas for another 30 minutes to set their shapes. Serve with steaming cups of coffee or chai (see page 253).

# Masala chai

Indians can not get enough of this spiced milk tea. It is drunk for breakfast, during tea time and at the end of meals, both for its delicious soothing effect and perceived medicinal properties. If you've ever tried the chai lattes served at the ubiquitous coffee chains around Britain, you should know that they're made with overly sweet, spiced syrup and are quite a contrast with the real thing!

Pour the water and milk into a saucepan and add the cardamom pods, peppercorns, cloves and cinnamon. Bring to the boil and then reduce the heat. Simmer gently for 12–15 minutes, stirring occasionally and ensuring that the milk does not boil over.

Add the tea bag and sugar to the pan and leave to infuse for a few minutes (depending on how strong you like your tea). Strain the liquid through a sieve and pour into two large mugs. Serve hot.

**SERVES 2**
500ml water
200ml whole milk
6 green cardamom
   pods, lightly crushed
3 black peppercorns
2 cloves
½ cinnamon stick
1 black tea bag
   (preferably Assam)
2 tsp caster sugar,
   or to taste

# Chai & Lightly spiced sesame cookies

**MAKES 20–25**

350g plain flour
¼ tsp baking powder
½ tsp fine sea salt
¼ tsp cardamom seeds,
  finely ground
60g sesame seeds
250g unsalted butter,
  softened
280g icing sugar
1 medium egg, lightly
  beaten
2 tbsp whole milk
60g unsalted cashew
  nuts

# Lightly spiced sesame and cashew nut cookies

Baked cakes, pastries and biscuits have not been traditionally eaten in India, as until recently many houses did not own ovens in their kitchens. However, many modern cooks are now making Western-style biscuits and cakes to be enjoyed at tea time. These tasty sesame and cashew nut cookies are ideal eaten with steaming cups of chai (see page 253). For dense and perfectly round cookies, leave out the baking powder but be sure to cream the butter and sugar well. A little baking powder makes for lighter cookies, but they do tend to spread out and flatten during baking.

Preheat the oven to 190°C/Fan 170°C/Gas 5. Sift the flour, baking powder, salt and cardamom into a large bowl and stir in the sesame seeds. In a stand-alone mixer, cream together the butter and sugar until light and fluffy. Gradually add the egg and milk. Using a low speed, add the flour mix, a little at a time, to form a stiff dough.

Place neat heaped spoonfuls of the cookie dough, about the size of golf balls, on to several greased baking trays, making sure the cookies are spaced well apart to allow for expansion. If there are little peaks on the cookies, pat them down lightly then top with a couple of cashew nuts. Bake for 20–25 minutes until the cookies are a pale golden brown colour.

Leave to cool a little before transferring the cookies to a wire rack. Cool completely before storing in an airtight container. They will keep well this way for about a week.

# Payasam

*Payasam* is a creamy rice pudding that is delicately flavoured with spices and chopped nuts. In addition to rice, it can also be made with wheat (popular in the north), lentils or vermicelli that has been boiled in mildly spiced, sweet milk. The dessert plays an essential part in wedding banquets and as offerings in Hindu temples. This recipe is based on the delicious payasam I ate in Kerala.

Put the rice, milk, water, jaggery or sugar and cinnamon into a medium heavy-based saucepan with a lid and bring to the boil. Reduce the heat to low, partially cover with the lid and leave to simmer gently for about 15–20 minutes, stirring every few minutes.

Add three-quarters of the chopped nuts and sultanas or raisins to the pan and stir well to combine. Remove the pan from the heat, cover with the lid and leave to stand for about 5 minutes. If the rice pudding becomes too dry, add a little boiling water.

Ladle the rice pudding into serving bowls, decorate with the remaining chopped nuts and sultanas and serve while still warm.

**SERVES 4–6**
150g basmati rice, rinsed and drained
400ml coconut milk (or whole milk)
400ml water
100g jaggery or light brown soft sugar
1 cinnamon stick, broken in half
50g mixed chopped nuts, such as blanched almonds, pistachio nuts and cashews
20g sultanas or raisins

**SERVES 4–6**

150g dried milk powder
75g plain flour
½ tsp baking soda
2 tbsp unsalted butter, melted
25–50ml whole milk
vegetable oil, for deep frying

**SUGAR SYRUP**

300g caster sugar
250ml water
2 tbsp rosewater

# Gulab jamon

These balls are northern Indian versions of round doughnuts, except that they are made with milk powder and drenched in a fragrant rosewater- or cardamom-infused syrup. Sometimes a pinch of saffron is added to the syrup to give it a golden tinge. The dessert is now widely enjoyed all over the subcontinent and is usually eaten during festivals and special celebrations. *Gulab jamon* is best eaten warm but it is also delicious at room temperature. It is important to soak the balls in the syrup straight after deep-frying so that they remain tender and moist.

To prepare the sugar syrup, put the sugar and water into a saucepan over a medium heat. Stir continuously to help the sugar dissolve, then bring to the boil and reduce the heat. Simmer gently for 10 minutes until reduced and slightly thickened. Stir in the rosewater and remove from the heat.

Tip the milk powder, flour and baking soda into a large bowl and stir to combine. Make a well in the centre, add the butter and stir in enough milk to bring the ingredients together to form a stiff dough. Let the dough rest for 20 minutes.

Divide the dough into 18–20 pieces and gently roll each piece in your hands to form a smooth ball. (Do not roll the balls too firmly as you want them to have a soft and light texture when cooked.) Place the balls on a large plate and cover with a damp tea towel.

Heat 6cm of oil in a deep, wide saucepan or karahi set over a high heat until hot, then turn the heat down to medium. Keep the heat at a constant medium-to-low temperature, about 110–130°C, and deep-fry the balls in batches. Add the balls to the pan one at a time. The balls will sink to the bottom of the pan so it is important to keep turning them to ensure an even golden brown colour all over. After about 3–5 minutes the balls will rise to the surface; at this point continue to cook slowly for a further 2–3 minutes until they are evenly golden brown.

Warm the syrup, then carefully remove the balls from the oil, drain on a plate lined with kitchen paper and place straight into the warm sugar syrup. (If you have time, leave the balls to soak in the syrup overnight and warm through gently before serving.)

# Cardamom and coconut-flavoured milk

This makes for a very soothing and flavourful drink, and I think it less cloying than a milkshake. You may want to reduce the amount of cardamom in the drink if you are serving it to young children, as they may not like the strong spice.

Tip the coconut into a blender, pour in the water and blend to a purée.

Place a saucepan over a medium heat and add the milk and sugar. Stir frequently to help the sugar dissolve, then add the coconut purée and crushed cardamom pods. Continue to heat until bubbles begin to form around the sides of the pan and the milk is almost boiling.

Immediately remove the pan from the heat and allow the cardamom and coconut to infuse for a further 20–30 minutes before straining through a fine sieve. Serve the flavoured milk warm or chilled.

**SERVES 4**
75g freshly grated
  coconut
75ml water
800ml whole milk
50g caster sugar
8–10 green cardamom
  pods, lightly crushed

# Rasmalai

This is a very popular dessert that originated in east India and Bangladesh. Essentially, it is small cottage-cheese dumplings that have been poached in sugar syrup then served with lightly infused sweet milk. Even though it will take a bit of time, you will get the best results if you make the cottage cheese yourself.

First, make the cottage cheese. Place a large muslin-lined sieve over a large bowl. Pour the milk into a saucepan set over a medium heat. As the milk begins to boil, add the lemon juice or vinegar and stir until the milk curdles. Pour the curdled milk into the muslin, tie up the sides and hang for 45 minutes–1 hour. Squeeze out any moisture using your hands. Knead the mixture until smooth, roll into 8–10 balls and flatten them slightly with your palm. Set aside on a plate.

To make the poaching syrup, put the sugar and water into a saucepan and stir until the sugar dissolves. Bring to the boil and cook for 5 minutes until thickened slightly. Reduce the heat to medium and carefully add the cottage-cheese balls to the pan. Partially cover the pan with a lid and poach the dumplings for 6–7 minutes. They will expand slightly when cooked. Remove the dumplings from the syrup and set aside. (The syrup can be strained and used to poach fruits.)

For the milk syrup, pour the milk into a wide saucepan and stir in the saffron, if using, pistachios, almonds, cardamom and rosewater. Bring to the boil. Reduce the heat slightly and cook, stirring, for 30 minutes or until the milk has reduced by a third. Stir in the sugar, and once it has dissolved add the dumplings. Simmer for a few minutes, remove the pan from the heat, cool completely and chill for a few hours. Divide among serving bowls and decorate with the toasted nuts.

**SERVES 4**
**COTTAGE CHEESE**
**DUMPLINGS**
1.5 litres whole milk
few drops lemon juice
 or malt vinegar

**POACHING SYRUP**
200g caster sugar
200ml water

**MILK SYRUP**
1 litre whole milk
pinch of saffron strands
 (optional)
1 tbsp chopped unsalted
 pistachio nuts
1 tbsp chopped
 blanched almonds
¼ tsp cardamom seeds,
 finely crushed
½ tsp rosewater
85g caster sugar

**TO DECORATE**
1 tbsp toasted pistachio
 nuts, roughly chopped
1 tbsp toasted almonds,
 roughly chopped

**SERVES 4**

2 litres whole milk
3–4 cardamom pods,
  seeds finely ground
130g caster sugar
1 tbsp rosewater
rose petals, to decorate
  (optional)

# Rosewater kulfi

*Kulfi* is the name given to traditional Indian ice cream. As a street snack, it is frozen in little tube-shaped terracotta pots and sold by vendors called *kulfi-wallahs* from large vats filled with crushed salted ice. Needless to say, the variety of flavours sold by such vendors is endless, but for a light and refreshing dessert I really like the subtle taste and fragrance of rosewater kulfi. It can easily be made at home and has the added bonus of not requiring an ice-cream machine, although if you have one feel free to churn the kulfi mixture to get a lighter, airy texture.

Pour the milk into a wide heavy-based saucepan and slowly bring to the boil. Turn down the heat, stir in the ground cardamom and simmer for an hour or until reduced by half. The milk must be stirred frequently to prevent it catching on the base of the pan and burning. If a skin forms over the milk, don't worry, simply stir it back in.

Once the milk has reduced, add the sugar and rosewater. Continue to simmer, stirring constantly, for 2–3 minutes until the sugar has dissolved. Remove the pan from the heat and leave to cool completely, stirring every once in a while to prevent a skin forming.

Pour the cooled milk into four kulfi or dariole moulds. Cover the moulds with cling film and carefully transfer to the freezer. Freeze for at least 6 hours or overnight.

To unmould the kulfis, dip the moulds briefly in a bowl of warm water and invert on to shallow serving bowls. Decorate with rose petals, if you wish, and serve immediately.

# Index

# Acknowledgements

This book would not have been possible without the support of my incredibly talented and dedicated team. First, I would like to thank Mark Sargeant and Emily Quah for their extraordinary dedication and their coordinated efforts in putting the book together, which include compiling and testing the recipes and styling the food for photography, Emma Lee and Jonathan Gregson for their amazing photography, Emma Thomas for her fantastic prop styling, Patrick Budge for designing yet another gorgeous and colourful book, and Emily Shardlow for her help with recipe testing.

My thanks also to the team at HarperCollins – Belinda Budge for her continued support; Hannah Black and Helena Caldon for their editorial work; and everyone involved in the production of this book.

I am also eternally grateful to the team at Optomen – from the dynamic Executive Producer, Pat Llewellyn, to the researchers, producers, cameramen, sound engineers and everyone else who worked tirelessly throughout the filming of the *Great Escape* episodes. My sincere gratitude also goes to all the remarkable individuals I met during my journey who have generously shared their time, knowledge and insights with me and shown me how to prepare truly wonderful, authentic and delicious Indian food.

My appreciation also to Jennifer Aves-Elliott, my PA, who has the admirable task of managing my diary and sorting out my life – a non-stop challenge not for the faint-hearted, I assure you. Also to my loving family and Chris Hutcheson for keeping me grounded and sane.

And finally, a special dedication goes to the late Alex Robinson – it was an honour to have known and worked with him and it would be an understatement to say that he will be deeply missed.

# Introduction

Over 3.5 million curries are eaten in the UK each year, which shows how much Indian cuisine is now part and parcel of the British diet. My own love affair with Indian food started when my mother made me my first curry as a child. Granted, mum's inauthentic curries were nothing like what we're used to today – hers were mostly flavoured with curry powder with the occasional handful of sultanas thrown in – but to us the flavours seemed exotic and mesmerising and I was hooked.